To all my friends and family, and all who have prayed for me.
You all helped me along the way and I thank God for you every day

Faith—
Through the storm

JEZ SMITH

AuthorHouse™
1663 Liberty Drive
Bloomington, IN 47403
www.authorhouse.com
Phone: 1-800-839-8640

© 2012 by Jez Smith. All rights reserved.

No part of this book may be reproduced, stored in a retrieval system, or transmitted by any means without the written permission of the author.

Published by AuthorHouse   03/19/2012

ISBN: 978-1-4678-9453-1 (sc)
ISBN: 978-1-4678-9454-8 (hc)
ISBN: 978-1-4678-9455-5 (e)

Any people depicted in stock imagery provided by Thinkstock are models, and such images are being used for illustrative purposes only.
Certain stock imagery © Thinkstock.

This book is printed on acid-free paper.

Because of the dynamic nature of the Internet, any web addresses or links contained in this book may have changed since publication and may no longer be valid. The views expressed in this work are solely those of the author and do not necessarily reflect the views of the publisher, and the publisher hereby disclaims any responsibility for them.

CONTENTS

CHAPTER 1	The Lord is my shepherd	1
CHAPTER 2	My grace is sufficient for thee, 2 Corinthians 12 verse 9	17
CHAPTER 3	A new angle of attack	29
CHAPTER 4	More grief	45
CHAPTER 5	Christmas 2008	57
CHAPTER 6	Vision of trouble ahead	65
CHAPTER 7	Sundays are for going out	85
CHAPTER 8	Back in church for the first time	95
CHAPTER 9	More heartache	107
CHAPTER 10	A new home	113
CHAPTER 11	Moving in and moving on	121
CHAPTER 12	The Lord is my strength	129
CHAPTER 13	Going home	135
CHAPTER 14	New beginnings	143
CONCLUSION		149

CHAPTER 1

THE LORD IS MY SHEPHERD

October 2008, the start of another busy month! I worked as a lorry driver delivering linen to hotels. My work took me all over Derbyshire and south Yorkshire, the work itself was heavy manual handling on a daily basis. Often requiring me to lift the linen up and down stairs at the hotels, Put on top of that running kids church on Sundays and being the father of two young children = life being always busy.

At the beginning of October I had no idea what was about to transpire but it would see me hospitalised, put through at times things that seemed unbearable, but see my walk with God deepen beyond anything I thought was possible!

I had begun that October feeling a little under the weather I remember in the week before I fell ill feeling really lethargic and as that week progressed I was really struggling at work, my energy levels seemed to be so low and I was almost willing the week to end so I could rest over the weekend. By the Sunday I was still not very well and stayed home from church, my wife was really concerned about me being ill but I told her I would be fine and sent her off to church with our two children. However my struggles continued and on Monday morning I was still no better and had to take a day off work and go to the doctors, he gave me some pills to take which by the Tuesday evening seemed to have sorted me out, so I rang my boss at work to tell him I would be back in work the next day.

Wednesday was always the busiest day of the week for me with lots of heavy deliveries and by mid morning I could tell that I had probably come back to work a day too early. My body felt so weak! It was the kind of feeling you get when you have had a really tough work out at the gym; everything afterwards just feels like such an effort. I struggled through the days work and felt so relieved when I finally arrived at my last Hotel to make the last delivery of the day. As I got out of the lorry I became really aware that my left leg was very tight around my calf muscle, the only way I can describe it is that it felt as though I had pulled a muscle and it was bad enough for me to be limping with it. I was really thankful that there was not a lot to deliver to this hotel and I was soon on my way back to my works depot.

I parked my lorry up in the compound at work and as I got out of the lorry I noticed that my limp had in fact gotten much worse, even though it had only taken me forty minutes to drive back. I limped my way into the office and my boss frowned at me and asked me what I had done. I told him I was not sure but told him that I had pulled a muscle in my leg and told him not to worry and that I would be in work the next day.

That evening my limp got even worse in fact it was no longer a limp it was now so bad I was tripping up over my left foot, my wife looked on as I struggled around the house on it with a worried look on her face. On Wednesday evenings our church holds small group bible studies. One week I would go and the next week my wife would go or if we had the money we would get a baby sitter for the evening and both go. Although every so often the study would take place at our house. That Wednesday it was my wife's turn to go, she was worried about leaving me at home with the children as I was struggling so badly but I told her that if I needed her I could ring her and get her to come home. Just after she had left I gave my baby daughter her last bottle of milk before taking her to bed. My leg was really bad now and just getting up the stairs holding my daughter in my arms was a struggle all of its own, the effort that it took just to do that was tremendous, something was not right but me being me I felt that I could struggle on. I went and checked on my son who was sound asleep so off I went back downstairs. With the children tucked up in bed I sat down for a few minutes trying to decide what to do, it was never much of a hard decision to make as I never really watched much TV as all it seemed to be filled with in the evenings was soap opera's. It was guitar for me, I had two guitars one acoustic and one electric the beauty of the electric was that I could play with my head phones on so not disturbing anybody else, plus people might not want to listen to the noise that I made with it anyway. I had been playing guitar for around one year after years of not playing and had had some lessons to help get myself back in to the groove.

A little later my wife came home and immediately asked me how my leg was, I told her it was no better and if anything it was worse than before. I still felt that a good nights sleep would make all the difference though. When my alarm went off the next morning I knew straight away that it was not good, in fact it was even worse than it had been the day before, my whole left leg now seemed to be dead and it felt like someone had tied a lump of lead to it. I struggled to get dressed and then went down stairs doing my best not to wake my wife and children up. Getting down stairs was a mission all of its own and the safest way seemed to be sat down, it seemed totally crazy I had not gone downstairs sat on my bottom since I was a child but here I was in my thirties reduced to having to get down that way. The unbelievable thing was that I still felt that after a quick hobble around downstairs I would be OK to go to work. I even made a sandwich and packed my work bag and on top of that hobbled up to my car only just able to weight bear through my left leg. God knows how stubborn I am and I truly thank him for what happened next, I got into my car and I tried to put the clutch down with my left leg, but it never happened! I just did not have the strength. I sat there a moment pondering over what had just happened or not as the case was and decided to have another go only to get the same result.

I just shook my head in disbelief. I rang my boss to tell him I would not be in work, when I explained to him what was going on, he sounded fairly worried and asked me to keep him informed as to how I got on at the doctors. So off to the doctors I went again for the second time that week, I had an appointment for eleven O, clock and without the ability to drive I had to rely on the bus, the nearest bus stop was about a five minute walk from my house but with a leg that was like dragging a lump of lead around it made that walk more like fifteen minutes. I arrived at the doctors with just about a minute to spare and had only just sat down when I heard the buzzer go indicating that one of the doctors at the surgery was ready for his next patient and yes it was for me. So I struggled back up onto my feet and limped through to his room.

My doctor was not used to seeing me twice in a year let alone twice in one week and I am no expert at reading body language but his tutting and shaking of his head told me he did not like what he was seeing, he performed various tests on my left leg most of them involving the use of his hammer trying to get a response from my nerves at the knee. Finally he was finished and asked me to take a seat. My doctor told me he was ringing the local hospital in advance and that he wanted me to go straight there so that they could investigate further what was happening. He asked me if I knew anyone who could take me to the hospital and I told him that I would ring around a few friends to see if anyone could help. I made my way back into the waiting room and I was met by my wife; she asked me straight away what the doctor had said and I could see the concern written all over her face when I told her he wanted me to go to hospital, as usual with me I told her I would be fine and that it was probably just a precaution. I asked my wife if she knew anybody who could take me to hospital and she said she would ring our friends house where she had just come from as the women had just met together for morning prayers. A few moments later she came back into the waiting room and told me Helen one of our friends would gladly take us.

After a short wait my doctor poked his head around the frame of the door and handed me a medical card, he told me that I needed to go to the accident and emergency department once I got to hospital and then book in with them and give them the medical card. My wife arranged for one of our other friends to pick our son up from school and after a quick pit stop at our house to pick up a few things for our daughter and some bits for me just in case I ended up spending more time in hospital than any of us thought I was going to; we were off. Helen was fantastic and I thanked her for dropping us off that afternoon, she had to dash off back to the estate we all lived on, to pick her eldest daughter up from school. I never really liked hospitals all the waiting around always drove me insane but that was going to have to change and very quickly, after seeing a nurse and explaining what was going on for what seemed the millionth time that day I had to then endure having my blood taken. I was never pleased about having needles stuck in me but I was very aware that they needed to take bloods to find out more about what was wrong with me.

After what seemed like another thousand years sat in the waiting room I was finally called through to be seen again this time by a doctor and once again I had to recite what had gone on. Followed by the same tests my doctor had performed on me back at the surgery, after the doctor had finished his examination he asked me to go and wait in the waiting room again. My wife looked really shattered and had already fed our daughter one bottle of milk in the time we had been at the hospital, I told her that if she needed to go I would be fine and would ring her the minute I knew anything, but my wife told me that she could hang on for a little while longer before ringing Helen who had already offered to pick us up when we needed to go home. Not that long after that I was called through by a nurse and I thought I was going to have to relay the events again, only to find that they were actually admitting me to a medical assessment ward at the hospital.

I should not really have been shocked but the longest I had ever spent in hospital was one night and that had only been for a routine operation on my left knee when I had been in the army so to suddenly find out that they thought I was ill enough to be admitted was quite a shock really. My wife looked more nervous than ever and really worried and I have to say that deep down I too was petrified. The date I arrived in hospital is etched in my memory like a wound you would rather forget about, the ninth of October 2008. This would be my first night away from my family and it was the scariest I had ever had, during my time serving in the armed forces I had seen active service and had experienced many dangerous incidents, but there I had always known what I was letting myself in for; this was the unknown, and I have to say this filled me with more dread and worry than anything I had faced before.

Saying goodbye to my wife and my baby daughter a little later was heart wrenching and it hurt me so much to know that my little boy was going to be going home that evening and I was not going to be there for him. I felt so sad that he was going to have to go through this. I knew that my wife was really hurting too and I could not comfort her either, it was a moment where I totally felt like a fish out of water. I had always been so strong but now my body seemed to be getting weaker and I did not know why. That first night in hospital was awful I felt so guilty and sad, I was cut off from my family and my only thoughts were how much they needed me. That night I prayed to God so many prayers over so many things I don't think I have ever had so much time in my life to just talk to God but I was making good use of the time I now had.

My whole body seemed to be getting weaker and I felt totally out of control. Just days earlier I had been fighting fit and healthy. No one had yet given me any indication of what they thought was wrong with me, but I was aware of how weak I was becoming and it was happening fast. When I had arrived on that ward I was able to get myself to the toilet which was only two bed spaces away from me but by the late evening I was needing a nurse to hold my left arm and give me some support so that I could make it there.

Whatever was wrong with me it was taking over my lower body, my legs were feeling very strange and hot and with a sensation of pins and needles. I was such a mess myself, I don't even recall what time I finally fell asleep or if I did get much at all but the next morning as I woke up I realised that I needed to go to the toilet so I called a nurse over to help me. As I began to swing my legs out of bed, I was instantly aware of how heavy they were. Yes I had described my left leg as being like a lump of lead but now it was both legs and they felt infinitely heavier than they had a day ago, in fact my left leg was so heavy now that I could not move it without having to use my arms to help.

I sat on the end of my bed and the nurse put his arm under my left arm to help me get up, I put all my effort into getting up but even with the help of a nurse I just could not do it the strength had simply gone and there was just no way I could get up. The nurse went off and came back a few minutes later with some strange bottle with a funnel on it, you will have to pee here he said and handed me the bottle and then closed the curtains around me, I have got to say that I was so embarrassed the nurses station was only a few feet away and there were women nurses sat there too. Its a stupid thing really to be embarrassed about! Nurses have seen I am sure every body shape and naked bit of flesh there is to see but that did not stop the way I felt as I sat there trying to work out how I was going to manage to do this whilst sat on my bed, however it did not take me that long to overcome my initial fears. I sat there feeling so fearful and simply could not understand where my strength had gone. As that morning went by and after explaining again and again to the ward doctors what was happening or as it was that less was happening the afternoon was soon upon me and visiting hours on the ward began and my wife arrived with my mum and stepfather. By that time other parts of my body were shutting down, it was like all the fuses were blowing one by one and there was no way of resetting them.

Me and my wife hugged each other, neither of us able to make any sense of what was happening. I did my best to put everyone's mind at rest telling them that I was sure I was going to be OK, but the honest answer was that as the day wore on and I continued to get weaker I felt more and more worried about what was happening to me. The doctor had not really been much help when I had asked him about it; he just told me that they were running blood tests to see what was wrong and that I should not worry as everything they could do was being done. The truth though is that your mind does wander and you end up thinking up all sorts of reasons why something like this might be affecting you I even blamed myself. Having been just days earlier fit and healthy this sudden loss of strength I was finding very scary and I have to say I had never felt such fear in my life.

Later that afternoon after my family had all gone home one of my friends came and paid me a visit and it just so happens that said friend is a doctor, Aidan immediately started looking over my charts on the end of my bed and asked me how I was. In myself I felt fine it was just this progressive weakness that was really worrying. Aidan told me he felt he knew what it was that I was suffering from and that although it was going to get worse he said that I should not worry as it was possible to recover from what he thought I had.

The condition he felt I had was called Guillain-Barre syndrome and yes I had never heard of it either. Aidan explained that the condition was very rare and only affects around one in a hundred thousand people a year, but that although it often completely paralyses those who suffer from it, it is possible to make a complete recovery from the condition. As we were talking and having a little bit of a joke with one another to lighten the mood he said to me, you know the ward sister don't you' I have to say I was not sure who the lady was but Aidan said, yes you do that's Susan from Mottram church! As I looked over to where Aidan was pointing I did recognise the lady he was pointing to, although if Aidan had not told me who it was I probably would not have known. So bad am I with putting names to faces, Aidan then went over and got Susan to come over and say hello. From that moment on I felt so much more at peace although I was away from my family God would not leave me alone for even a moment. What was happening was dreadful and was really worrying but God was making sure that I was surrounded by his beautiful people here on earth, God himself had placed me into the care of these people.

That night as I lay in bed muscles in my back were twitching away like mad, it felt as though they were having a party and I knew that they were just shutting down. Every moment that went by I was getting less and less mobile in fact I don't recall the last time I had spent a whole twenty four hours in bed but one thing was for sure, I was going to have to get used to it as it looked like I was going to be like this for some time yet. A doctor came to see me that evening and told me that he had scheduled me in for an MRI scan on the Monday morning, I immediately asked him why I was having to wait until the Monday to have the scan; but he just told me that it was because the MRI department was fully booked up until then. One of the things Aidan had told me was that it was really important that the condition got diagnosed quickly otherwise it really could complicate things. I could not help feeling that Monday could be too late, I lay there in bed on the ward praying and feeling like I was letting my family down by being ill, its not something I can explain easily but I really felt awful. I felt as though a storm was raging all around me tossing me here and there and the only safety I could find was Jesus and I felt as though I was hanging on for dear life.

    I woke up on my third day in hospital to find that I could no longer sit myself up, I was now only able to move my head and my eyes. The rest of my body had now shut down and I mean everything. I was no longer able to control any muscles below my head and I needed medical intervention for bodily functions. Everything that we do in our every day lives was now being done by nurses on the ward for me. I was being spoon fed and washed by them, I was shaved by nurses, dressed by them. It was like digressing back to being a baby with the level of care I now required. I was now completely dependant on the care of all the staff on that ward, it did not matter what it was that needed doing they now had to do it. Having an illness that strips everything away from you really makes you appreciate every little thing the body does, I would lie there watching my hands intently to see if I could make them move, but they were completely still.

    That Saturday I had many visitors, my wife came with my two children and it was so lovely to see them, I had not seen my son since the day I was taken into hospital and just to be able to reassure him myself seemed really important, the poor little lamb looked so scared I really felt for him. I chatted with my wife and her concern for what was happening was in every word that she spoke. She genuinely seemed to be struggling to hold herself together with all that had happened in such a short space of time. I did not know what to say and I felt so helpless, my wife was really scared and nothing I could say helped in any way. I had never been in a situation where things were outside of me being able to control them, I remember crying for the first time that afternoon but such were my physical problems I could not even wipe away the tears welling in my eyes and my wife had to do it for me. I even told her I was sorry and she told me that I had nothing to be sorry for. The emotional side of this illness really is a roller coaster and it is hard to put into words the range of emotions that I was going through. All I could feel was that I was letting people down. Many of my friends from church visited me that afternoon, some prayed with me, some did not know what to say but for me just knowing that they genuinely cared and were praying was all I needed to know. Seeing them taking time out of their lives to come and visit me was really special and I thank God for the love they were all pouring out upon my family. My mum and stepfather visited me again that afternoon, they had phoned around all of the family to let them know what had happened and my mum informed me that she had spoken to my dad and that he was planning to come up and visit me as soon as he could.

My dad had moved to London a couple of years earlier to live with his new wife and taken a job down their after years of working at the same place in Manchester, he now worked at a church in London and I have to say it was the perfect job for my dad. I was told that afternoon by Jim the pastor of our church that that evening the church were holding an evening of prayer for me, I felt so blessed and loved by everybody and it was very humbling. He told me that one of the specific things they were praying for was that I would be moved to another hospital. The hospital that I was at was a general hospital and in all honesty my friend Aidan the doctor really felt that I needed to be moved to Hope hospital in Salford where they had wards that specialised in caring for patients with my suspected illness. Visiting hours end so soon and Jim prayed with me just before he left, I don't know why but just as he was leaving I asked him what time they were meeting to pray for me and he told me it was eight in the evening the information was really of no use to me but it just felt nice to know.

I was soon alone again, just me the nurses and other sick patients along with machines that on the face of it their primary function was just to bleep all day and night long to annoy people. All I had were my thoughts and God, never in my life had I spent so much time just praying and spending time with him, but I found such strength and peace in him and everything that was happening should have left me a complete wreck and yet I lay there in my hospital bed feeling calm, at peace and suddenly with no fear. God had some how just given me such inner courage and his presence I could certainly feel. Some people say that they fear death and would not know how to react if they found themselves facing what I was at that moment, but that is the beauty of knowing Jesus, not having to fear death I knew who my lord and saviour was. Psalm 56 verse 4: In God I will praise his word, In God I have put my trust; I will not fear what flesh can do unto me.

That evening a doctor came to see me and told me that I was being transferred to Hope hospital in Salford. I looked over at the clock on the wall near the nurses station and almost let out a laugh, it was just a few minutes after eight in the evening; moments earlier my friends would have begun to pray to God for the very move that I was soon to undertake. The Lord listens to our prayers never does he forsake us, he is full of grace and love for his children. It was about half an hour later when the ambulance crew arrived to take me up the motorway network to Hope hospital. They lined up their stretcher next to my bed and then put what they called a pat slide under my right side and with the help of a couple of nurses they slid me across to their stretcher. They then put straps across me and buckled them down, I had no intentions of falling off their stretcher but I suppose it is better to be safe than sorry. Just before they took me off the ward I asked one of the nurses if she would ring my wife to let her know that I was being transferred to Hope hospital, she told me that it would be her next job. Being strapped to a stretcher does put the funniest things in your mind I suddenly thought about the film The silence of the lambs and how Hannibal Lector was transported from one secure prison to another on a stretcher, all I needed was a mask over my mouth. Yes I guess three days of being in hospital had already begun to let my mind wander a little. Soon we were on our way to Salford and the journey took about thirty minutes, I was really glad when we finally did arrive at what was about to become my new home for a few months. First off the ambulance was freezing, I was sure the crew had never heard of vehicle heaters and secondly I do not ever recall having to look at the ceiling of a vehicle for such a stretch of time before in my life.

The guys got me out of the ambulance and swiftly began to wheel me through brightly lit corridors as we made our way to the ward that was about to become my home for about two months. we finally arrived at the door of the ward and I was then wheeled into a room that had three other male patients in it. The ward that was now my new home was the acute neurological unit or ANU for short, I was then yet again man handled across into the bed that they had allocated for me and then it was time to meet the staff. The ward sister was standing by the far end of my bed space

Faith—Through the storm

near the window and he introduced himself "Hi I am Ollie" he said "and this is your nurse for tonight Karen" after saying hello to them both and meeting my new room mates it was down to business Ollie asked me how I was and went through the general questions they ask new patients. He finished with a question that must have always bothered him as I saw in his face that he had all too often heard the answer No! "so Jez have you any religious beliefs"? when I answered "yes I am a Christian" his face lit up and he told me he was too, I again knew that God had put me in a place where I was in his care and it was such a comfort to know that.

He and Karen then left me to settle in a moment but I did not get too much time as moments later it was the turn of the ward doctor she came in and asked me all the same questions that I had now answered goodness knows how many times. She then explained what was going to be going on, I would shortly be whisked off to have a CT scan and then later when I was back on the ward I would have a lumber puncture done on my spine. Karen accompanied me through the hospital corridors and lifts to the CT department and then stayed with me while I had the test done. The test seemed to take forever and was not the most comfortable thing in the world to find yourself in. It was like being shoved down a torpedo launch tube not that I ever had been down one but I now had a good idea what it felt like and the noise was unbelievable. We were soon done and had to wait around for the porters to come and take us back to the ward. If I thought that the CT scan was uncomfortable I was about to find out what truly being uncomfortable meant! As soon as I arrived back on the ward the doctor was ready to perform the lumber puncture. She had forewarned me that this would be the worst of the tests they needed to carry out that evening but that it was necessary so that they could diagnose what was wrong with me. Karen rolled me onto my side so that the doctor could get on with the procedure, Karen promised me a nice piece of toast and a cup of tea at the end of the procedure and that sounded like a great idea to me, it had been a long night so far and I was already feeling tired from all the different procedures I had been through that night.

I felt the doctor push the needle into my back, it was extremely uncomfortable and I could feel the needle digging deep into my spine. I certainly would not choose to have it done if I was given a choice but I was just going to have to endure it being done. I don't know how long the lumber puncture took to do but eventually it was all done and I was rolled back onto my back, Karen left the room after asking me how I like my tea and I began to take in my new surroundings, the room I was in had five bed spaces in it. My own being in the bottom corner on the left side of the room near the window, on the opposite side of the room their were three bed spaces and all were occupied. Two of the guys were asleep but the one directly opposite me was still awake watching his TV. He said hello but not a lot more but I had already noticed that he seemed to be like a jack in a box as every few minutes he was up and down. Karen soon arrived back with my cup of tea and some toast and I loved every mouth full of it, although I did feel awful as Karen had to stand there the whole time and feed it all to me. I was now also struggling with cups so was having to use a straw to drink through which was a whole new experience with hot drinks. I soon finished my late night treat and Karen made me comfortable and switched my bed side light off, she was about to leave the room when the man across from me got up again she swiftly turned around and told him, Zach if you keep getting up I will have to put a nurse in here with you all night! So that was his name! At that Zach thought better of it and got straight back in bed. It was now time to catch some sleep if I could, I was already beginning to realise that my new friend across from me was quite the night owl but eventually I did drift off.

    A few hours later I woke up, it was now two in the morning and I was in agony my back felt as though someone was trying to drill right through it, Karen had done her best to put my call bell near my head so that I could ring for assistance by basically nutting it with my head, the one time I needed it, it had moved in my bed and I could no longer reach it so I was going to have to do it the old fashioned way and just call out for a nurse. I felt bad about calling out as there was no two ways about it, I was going to end up disturbing the other guys in my room but I was in so much pain I needed some pain relief. I called out a couple of times and watched on painfully as the other guys began to be disturbed from their sleep, thankfully just moments later Karen came in to the room, "Thank God"! I explained how much pain I was in and asked if their was anything she could give me to help. She told me that the only thing she could give me was paracetamol as they had not yet got me on any specific medication as the doctor needed to prescribe it, to be honest I was just thankful that I was going to get something that would help.

    Karen scooted off and reappeared a few minutes later with said paracetamol and some other device in hand, she helped me take the pain relief tablets and then showed me the device in her hand and explained to me what it was. She told me that it was a flow meter, it was a device that measures the strength of how much air you can exhale from your lungs with a deep breath. She went on to tell me that with the condition I was suspected of having that one of the problems often faced is that you end up having breathing difficulties as the condition takes over your body. She set the machine up and then asked me to make a seal with my lips around it and then give it my all. I sucked in as much air as I could and then blew out with all my might, Karen took the machine and then read the reading off of it. Good she said as she put the reading onto a chart at the end of my bed, I was rather inquisitive and asked how well I had done, you scored four point eight she replied which is good considering that you have been immobile for a few days. I was now hooked and asked her what generally healthy people scored, she twisted her face a moment deep in thought and then said roughly five to six litres so your not doing badly at the moment. Karen then made me comfortable again and told me to try and get some sleep.

My bed in itself was quite annoying as I had to have a air mattress which hummed all the time and was constantly moving around underneath me, it was something that was necessary with me being totally immobile though as there was a big chance of me getting pressure sores and the skin could begin to break down so I was just going to have to get used to it. I lay there awake for a good while waiting for the pain relief to kick in, and after what must have been at least an hour I finally fell asleep.

I was woken at five in the morning by the ward doctor, "sorry to wake you so early" she said "but I have just got your test results back and I can confirm that you are suffering from Guillain-Barre syndrome" she went on to tell me what treatment they were going to give me. Something called immunogloblin which would be intravenously fed into the blood stream. She told me that she was going off to sort the medicine prescription out and that Karen would be in to fit a intravenous tap. Sure enough a few moments later Karen arrived ready to stick yet another needle into my arm. Karen had again brought the flow meter with her to check how my lungs were doing explaining that unfortunately I was going to have to get used to having it taken every few hours from now on as they needed to keep a close eye on how I was doing. The reading was roughly the same so she left the room looking pleased and I now had a new game to play as I was already becoming a little obsessive about what reading I was getting.

It was not long after that, that Karen arrived with the bottle and another machine on a stand, this machine helped feed the medicine into the body and I watched on with interest as she set it all up, she attached the feeding tube to my intravenous tap and then set the machine off. I now had yet another thing to annoy me as this thing clicked every few moments and was like having a chicken clucking next to my head all the time.

Karen explained to me what the immunogloblin did, basically its job was to shut my immune system down as it was my own immune system that was attacking my body, she also explained that each bottle cost around three hundred pounds and that I had to have three bottles of it a day for a whole week and telling me with a cheeky grin on her face that at the end of the course of treatment that I would be worth as much as a small car.

Guillain-Barre syndrome is a inflammatory disorder in which the body's immune system attacks the peripheral nerves. Severe weakness and numbness in the legs and arms characterise GBS. Loss of feeling and movement (paralysis) may occur in the legs, arms, upper body and face. Severe cases may result in total paralysis and breathing difficulties, requiring long term rehabilitation. With as many as 15% experiencing lasting physical impairment. In some cases, GBS can be fatal. Because the cause of GBS is unknown there is no way to prevent the disease from occurring. The condition takes over very quickly and seems to always creep up the body from the lower extremities usually beginning in the feet, the condition affects around one in a hundred thousand people a year and is a rare condition, the exact cause of Guillain-Barre syndrome is not known however in most cases the person affected will have had a virus or bacterial infection a few weeks before the condition sets in. Most people who suffer from Guillain-Barre syndrome make a full recovery within a few weeks or months and have no further problems, however some people may take longer to recover and there is a possibility of permanent nerve damage.

Having this stuff pumped into my veins was not nice either, whatever it was it really made me feel weird and on top of that the aches and pains I was now experiencing were excruciating the staff were now regularly coming in to move me into a new position which would make me comfortable for only about half an hour before I would ask if they could move me again, the staff never complained about having to come and try and make me comfortable although they did joke that if I kept being a pest they would put me in a cupboard out of the way, which always made me laugh.

Job 2 verse 7

So went Satan forth from the presence of the Lord, and smote Job with sore boils from the sole of his foot unto his crown.

I may not have had sores from my feet to the top of my head like Job did, but the pain I was so often in was just horrendous, the doctors were prescribing new pain relief almost daily to try and bring it under control. My elder brother Paul asked why they did not give me morphine, but the answer was they could not because one of the side affects of morphine is that it makes your breathing laboured, so it was far too dangerous to give me with a illness that already affects your breathing. My breathing was now showing signs of not being as strong as it had been during the first day on the ward but was not yet so bad that the staff were concerned. It was lovely to see my brother and my mum that Sunday afternoon, one thing that was really bothering me was feeling really stiff and whilst visitors were there with me I would often ask that they moved my legs for me. My brother was glad I think to be able to do something for me and the relief that something so simple brought to me was wonderful. Being in hospital gave you such small amounts of time with your loved ones and I was always was sad when they had to go, I always tried to be strong for them as I did not want them seeing me at my worst when the pain took over.

That evening when my wife arrived she told me how much everyone was rallying around and that she was going to be able to see me every evening as the church had drawn up a list of people who were going to bring her to see me, I was so humbled by the love and support that we as a family were being given. With the ward being a acute ward it meant that my children were not allowed to come onto the ward, it broke my heart that I could not see them, but I also understood the reasons why. There were a lot of very poorly people on this ward and I did worry how my son would react to just seeing me ill let alone anyone else. This also meant that for my wife to come and see me she needed a baby sitter to look after the children and again our friends from church stepped in and filled the breach for us, their love was just pouring out and at times it was so overwhelming. My wife was often very emotional when she came to see me and I am sure that seeing her husband just cut down like this was very difficult to deal with plus having to manage at home with the children and for me knowing that there was nothing I could do to help was really hard.

I think that probably hurt the most for me, I had always been so strong and now I was anything but that.

By the Tuesday of that first week I became aware of just how rare my illness was as I was now the wards favourite patient for medical students and their lecturers and I would end up with a host of students crowded around my bed whilst their lecturer got them to work out what I was suffering from, it was interesting watching them work it out. I also had one more test done that week, this time checking the nerve conductivity in my arms which basically meant being hooked up to electrodes to test them. So I was wheeled around onto another ward where a doctor performed the test on me from my bed. He did say that it would not hurt but that I should feel a mild pain in my arms, well I had news for him it did hurt! This test was always done with people who were suffering from Guillain-Barre syndrome it was usually just to confirm that the nerves were not reacting, and sure enough there was no reaction from my nerves, confirming my illness further.

Through those first few days the lord had been so close to me I knew he was watching over me, carrying me and I could feel his comfort. his love was just pouring out upon me. Everything had been stripped away, But the truth is that I could feel the Lords presence and as PSALM 23 says, The Lord is my shepherd, I shall not want.

Everything in me should have been going insane yet I was feeling calm and at peace and with all the love being pored out through our church and other churches, it all just showed me how much God was looking after me and my family. God's care for me was very apparent. I had already in just a few days met at least seven members of staff who were also Christians and I truly felt that it was no mistake that God had placed me in their care.

CHAPTER 2

MY GRACE IS SUFFICIENT FOR THEE, 2 CORINTHIANS 12 VERSE 9

By Tuesday night the nurses had stepped up the amount of times they were monitoring my ability to breath, as the day had wore on it had gotten steadily worse. I was not yet critical or so bad that they were calling for a doctor but they were concerned enough that on a few occasions I was asked to retake the test. Just doing the test once was exhausting enough and I really had to gear myself up to do it, but the results were getting worse each time. I did not really get much sleep that Tuesday night as I was now being woken every hour and a half and in all honesty the pain I was in was still not under control. I was often calling for a nurse to see if there was anything they could give me to help with it, only to be told that I would have to wait another couple of hours, the nurses were fantastic though and would come in and move me into another position to see if it would help alleviate the pain, sometimes It did but usually only for a short space of time often I would be on the brink of falling asleep when pain would just start nagging at me and eventually it would get so bad that I could no longer cope with it and I would end up calling for a nurse. I could see the frustration on their faces when they came in to tend to me for what would often be the umpteenth time that they had done so that night, but they were so understanding the only problem I truly had was that once they had made me comfortable it would often not be long before they were back again to check my breathing.

I woke from what little sleep I did get on Wednesday morning when the lights all flickered on around the ward, this was always a sign that the night shift had gone home and had now been replaced on the ward by the morning shift. Just minutes later the health care assistants would come into the room to start getting us all ready for breakfast. As I was bed ridden this meant me having a wash in my bed each morning and this required two nurses each day. The whole process usually took around ten minutes after which they would ask me what I wanted for breakfast, there was the usual variety of cereals and of course toast if you fancied it or porridge, as a general rule I was a weetabix man but occasionally I would go for the toast or the porridge. Mike was the duty nurse that morning and he came in shortly after breakfast with the drugs trolley to give us all our morning med's. This meant me again having to have my breathing assessed and as Mike fed me my pills giving me a suck on a straw for some water he remarked that he had heard what a bad night I had had. I nodded my head as I swallowed. In fact I was feeling exhausted and was so drained, Mike set the flow meter up and then asked me to blow as hard as I could. I mustered what strength I could and then gave it my best shot. Mike did not look overly impressed with the reading and asked me to do it again. So I tried again this time screwing my face up as though it could somehow help get more air out of my lungs, it was a slightly better result the second time around and Mike said "that's a little better but its not good" I asked him what the reading was, not now because I found it an interesting game but because now I was aware that things were getting serious. Mike told me that I had scored a little over two litres! When I had settled down to go to sleep the night before I was still scoring over three litres and through the course of the night it had gotten steadily worse, but this score was a dramatic drop from the last one that I had done!

As that Wednesday morning went by the results continued to drop with my breathing and by the the time afternoon visiting began I was feeling really tired, I was not sure if I would be getting any visitors that afternoon but as the clock ticked past two my mum walked into the room flanked by my two brothers. They brought news that our dad was going to be coming up to see me and would probably be up that weekend, I just nodded my head in response. I was so shattered that I kept closing my eyes while they were with me, my mum on a few occasions told me that if I needed to sleep I should not worry. But I was not letting that happen they had come all this way to see me and they did not want to be around someone who was asleep. To be honest though I am sure I was not much company for them as I said so little while they were there, but I was pleased to see them. It always touched me when people came to see me but all too soon visiting hours would be over again and they would have to leave, my mum kissed me goodbye and said she would be up again on Friday.

One of the things that each bed space did have was its own television on an arm that swung over your bed in front of you the only down side with them was that they needed topping up via a card so that you could watch them, and I could not believe how expensive they were. Five pounds got you roughly two days viewing. My wife had bought me a card on the Sunday but that had already run out, so my elder brother paid for another one that Wednesday afternoon. As was always the case for me it meant someone else setting up the TV and putting on something that I fancied watching, but it would not be long before I would be asking a nurse if they could change the channel for me. One thing I did realise very quickly though was that my taste for enjoying the tv had not changed, the only problem I had now was that I could not do anything else, so I would have to embrace it to some degree.

That evening my wife arrived with two of our friends from church Janet and Geraldine and they asked me how I was, Geraldine bless her had bought a small teddy from one of the shops at the hospital and put it on my side unit telling me that he would help keep me safe, the thought was very blessing and I thanked her for it. My wife did her best to bring me news of how well the children were doing, telling me that our son was despite everything that was going on was doing great at school and that my daughter was starting to try and crawl, it really hurt to be parted from them and I told my wife how much I missed her and the children.

Whilst my wife and friends were there a nurse came to check my breathing, I put every ounce of effort into getting as good a reading as I could and once again was asked to do it again, I was feeling so shattered though and this time I got the same score. The nurse told me that they needed to go and talk to the staff nurse who was on duty that evening. My wife looked really concerned as did our friends and just a few moments later Ollie came in to see me, "Jez he said "I am ringing through to the intensive care ward that reading is really bad you only scored one point three and if it drops any further you will have to be ventilated so I am ringing through to have you transferred into their care." Intensive care! whoa this was getting serious, I lay there in my hospital bed feeling so anxious I was so worried and I could see the worry on the face of my wife, whilst we were waiting for the porters to come our two friends said they needed a brew so left me and my wife alone for a short while. We had had so little time together since I fell ill and just to feel my wife holding my hand was so nice. Guillain-Barre was such a strange illness I could not move at all but I was able to feel even the slightest touch even on my toes and now as I waited fear really gripped me. Up until this point I had felt secure, that everything was going to be fine but I was now so worried and wondered if things could get any worse. Being told that I would have to be ventilated if my breathing got ant worse really had put fear into me.

A short while later the porters arrived and even though visiting hours had finished the staff on the ward had allowed my wife and friends to stay with me until I was transferred up to the intensive care ward and were also allowed to accompany me up in the lift and wait with me while a bed space on the ward was prepared for me. After what seemed an eternity a nurse finally came round to the corridor section of the ward where I was to move me onto the ward, I remember her telling my wife and friends that they would have to go to a waiting room before being allowed to say goodbye to me as they had a lot to do. I was wheeled onto the main ward, this room was very different from the ward I had come from, for starters it was open plan and all the patients were in one room. I was wheeled right up the room and into the bottom corner next to the nurses rest room. The nurse who was caring for me told me that a doctor was coming to see me and that he would be along soon. She also said that visiting time was now over so she was going to let my wife come over and say good night and then her and our friends would have to go. My wife came over said goodnight and then went home, I began to look around my new surroundings every bed space had an array of machines that were all bleeping, this was the serious end of the hospital but to be honest my recollection of it is very hazy, I was just so shattered and had very little energy.

The doctor finally arrived and he looked none too pleased, the first thing he commented on was my face "when did that begin"? he said' I was not sure what he was going on about, he replied that my face had dropped on one side which he called a bells palsy and he felt that it was strange as in his estimation the chances of me having a stroke on top of the illness I already had were extremely remote. This led him to perform all the tests that all the other doctors I had seen had already performed and by the end of his thorough examination he was satisfied that the loss of movement in the left hand side of my face was just in fact due to the Guillain-Barre just continuing to spread, although he was surprised about that as I had now been on the immunogloblin for nearly four days and he felt that by now that should be stopping it from continuing to spread.

One thing that was still a major problem for me was pain control and I told the doctor that I was still in agony despite the array of different med's I was now on. He looked at my notes and after some careful consideration he put me on a new drug on top of those I was already taking he told me that it may be a few days before I would feel the benefits of the drug but he hoped that it would bring my pain under control. He also informed me that he was getting the on call physio to come and see me and they were going to do some work on my breathing. After he left the nurse came back who was assigned to care for me that night and began to hook me up to all the various machines. I lay there afterwards thinking to my self that if ever I looked like Frankenstein now was the moment the only advantage I had was that I did not need zapping to be alive.

The nurse had also hooked me up to oxygen and the feeling of sure relief was overwhelming, the strange thing was that before the nurse turned it on I was just so out of touch with how much I was struggling for my breath. But now I was getting what seemed like huge amounts of air and I quickly began to feel like I was so much better. I had not been hooked up to the machines that long when the physio arrived she was pulling a contraption behind her that had a long hose wrapped around it, "hi she said, my name is Laura and this is the bird" she said pointing to the machine she had pulled along with her on its squeaky wheels. I commented that it did not look like it was a good flyer' she grinned at me and replied "I see you are a comedian." She then went on to explain what the bird did and that basically its job was to fill my lungs up to capacity and then let them deflate when they were full. She explained the technique to me that I would need to do and it sounded simple enough. I basically needed to create a seal around the mouth piece and then begin to suck in and then when I felt I had enough just stop and the machine would do the rest. Although the machine did a lot of the work whilst we did this I found it truly exhausting and was glad when Laura told me we were finished. Before she left she gave my chest a good massage, I say a good massage but the truth was that it really hurt she told me that she needed to do it as it would help to keep my chest clear and hopefully after a few sessions of this each day my breathing would stabilise. After a short period of torture Laura told me that she had finished. She then hooked me back up to the oxygen and told me to rest telling me that it would probably be a different physio that came to see me the next day who would put me through the same torture she had just inflicted upon me, how I was not looking forward to that!

Unknown to me on that evening when I was being transferred to intensive care one of the reasons our two friends went to get a drink was that they took time to pray for me and wanted to call our pastor Jim to inform him of what was happening. On that particular evening he was running a freedom in Christ course, on receiving this phone call Jim relayed the message to those present on the course and everybody stopped and instead prayed for me that evening.

2 Corinthians 9 verse 14, and in their prayers for you their heart will go out to you, because of the surpassing grace God has given you.

That night I did not sleep all that much again, I had tubes here and there and the new pain relief had not yet really kicked in although I did feel more comfortable for longer periods. At some point in the night one of the sticky pads on my chest came off and the machine behind me went berserk which in turn brought every nurse on the ward rushing towards me, as the first nurse arrived I told her that one of the pads had come off, she relayed the message to the other on rushing members off staff and immediately a sense of calm suddenly replaced the madness that had just moments earlier begun. My nurse came and got a new pad to stick down in place of the one that had just come off, she joked that I must have done that on purpose! I smiled as best I could a little lopsided but I tried. As she was there she said that we may as well check my breathing with the flow meter, I thought that I might get away with that for a while now I was on oxygen, once done the nurse told me that there had been no change in the reading. The thought of being ventilated was a scary one I was in my own mind anyway giving my all to fight this illness, if only my body responded to will power alone I would have been up and running around already and as I lay there unable to sleep most of the night I prayed for God to intervene.

Thursday morning seemed to come upon me so soon, it had been a chaotic night and I doubted that in a place like this I was going to get much sleep at all, the one thing I was glad of though was that it was not as blisteringly hot as the ward I had come from. ANU was so hot that I was living most days in just the most minimal amount of clothing the ward would allow, I truly felt that the Sahara desert was probably quite Wintry by comparison.

Despite how little sleep I seemed to have gotten that night I some how felt refreshed, I felt so at peace I knew that God had done something amazing that night and some how, Gods holy presence was all around me and he was filling me with a deep joy despite the obvious seriousness of the situation I was in. I can not truly explain how I could feel like that yet I knew that God had listened to prayer and had placed his peace and comfort directly into my heart that night. That morning when my new nurse arrived my breathing was yet again assessed, she told me that for now my breathing seemed to have stabilised though it was not yet improving.

A doctor came to see me later that morning and told me that he was pleased so far with the response I had made overnight to the treatment they had given me. He told me that although my breathing was stable and was showing the same consistent score each time it was checked that if it began to deteriorate again then it was most likely they would have to put me into a induced coma and I would be on full life support. The idea of having to go through that as well did not sound very good, but so much had already happened and I knew that God was watching out for me, one of the things that I was clearly hearing from God was that I must trust him and that whatever needed to be done by the staff I was just going to have let them do. In all honesty being paralysed from the neck down did leave you totally at the mercy of the staff anyway but in God I was trusting.

My nurse for that morning had asked me if I had anything to occupy my time as there were no televisions on this ward, with all the equipment around the beds there was just no room and to be honest most of the patients were asleep most of the time anyway. Geraldine who had come to see me the night before had brought me a CD player to use and some music to listen to but that was still on ANU. My nurse told me that she had to go down there anyway to talk to the doctors and nurses on that ward so she told me that she would pick it up while she was there. An hour or so later she came back with the CD player in hand, there were a few CD's to choose from but I was just glad to have something to listen to. The only down side to it was that the ear pieces occasionally fell out of my ears so leaving me listening to a very tinny version of the songs on the CD's, but it was a great relief from the constant bleeping of machines.

Lunch time was fast approaching and a nurse came over to me, she told me that my pastor from church had arrived to see me and asked me if it was OK for him to come in and I was fine with that. She told me he would not be allowed to stay for very long as it was outside of visiting hours and then went to get him. I looked over to the wards door waiting for him to appear, I was a little surprised when Gareth came through the door but was very pleased to see him and beckoned him over with a nod of my head just about the only movement I could still perform. He immediately asked me how I was, and I told him I was fine considering the circumstances, he explained that Jim would have come to see me but he was away on a course so he had asked Gareth if he would come to see me, Gareth said "he hoped I did not mind" and of course I did not. Gareth by rights was the pastor of our sister church in Mottram but he was still hugely involved in our church as he had helped plant our church around five years before.

He shared with me how everyone was holding me in prayer and how they were looking out for my wife and children. Hearing these things was always so humbling and gave me such great encouragement, Gareth however told me that I was a great encouragement to him in the way that I was dealing with my illness and yet I myself did not understand how or why. To be an encouragement felt somehow foreign to me yet it was something many people had already told me during my time in hospital already. One verse that truly speaks to me on this is Luke 9 verse 23, if any man will come after me, let him deny himself and take up his cross daily and follow me.

I truly felt as though the whole experience of being ill like this and having so many things just stripped away so suddenly was like having a Job like experience. Particular verses in the book of Job would flash through my mind as I lay in hospital, one of those verses was Job 2 verse 9 and 10, are you still holding on to your integrity curse God and die, he replied you are talking like a foolish woman shall we accept good from God and not trouble.

I knew that God would always be there for me and it would do me no good to curse him for what was happening to me the only thing I could do was to take up the cross given to me, for me there was no question in my mind about the strength that God was giving me to get through this and as I have said I could feel his love so strongly. I could feel God carrying me and caring for me, but sometimes we have to face things that truly test our faith and God allows these things so that we will become mature and more complete. At any time we can decide to reject God and try to do things in our own strength and turn to another path but I knew the path that I wanted to be on for I know my saviour and often when we truly walk with God is when we truly face our sternest tests. For we have an enemy who does not want us to be saved he wants us for himself and will try any trick he can to take us away from Gods love and salvation. I felt like I was living out that moment in the book of Job where Satan is given authority to do his worst against Job but must spare his life and I found Job a great inspiration for dealing with my own illness and separation from my family.

Gareth had been with me a good half hour when the dinners arrived on the ward and he said he would go, but one of the nurses said that if I was OK with it Gareth could feed me my lunch, he asked me if I was OK with that and it sounded like a great idea to me, I lay there almost chuckling to myself as Gareth went to get the tray of food not so much at the thought of one of my friends feeding me my dinner but at the irony of it. Here was Gareth used to feeding his parishioners the food of the bible and yet just for today it would be a beef dinner very different food indeed. I think that Gareth would say that it goes down as maybe the only moment he has ever quite so literally fed one of his parishioners. Once lunch was finished he prayed with me before he had to leave, I thanked him for his time but he replied, no thank you Jez its been a privilege.

Not long after lunch the physio;s arrived, two of them this time to give me my daily dose of torture so yet again I got myself acquainted with the bird and went through all the breathing exercises again, before yet another session of having my chest beaten and massaged. The bird had now become a new occupant of my bed space on the ward and I wondered if it was at all possible to get any more pieces of equipment around my bed, but I sure was not going to ask for any. The hope of the physio;s was that by using the bird daily I would not need to be ventilated. During my first few days in Hope hospital I had met the physio and occupational therapist's that worked on ANU and they had given me some leg splints, they told me that they were primarily to stop my muscles shortening. These things looked like a pair of boots only they were bright blue in colour and my toes stuck out of the end of them. I hated wearing them as they were very uncomfortable on my legs as they often brought on cramps and pains, so I would try telling the staff that I did not need them on, not that they often listened to me.

One other thing that had happened was that when I had lost all movement my hands had curled up and were almost fully in a fist shape, so between the physio and occupational therapist's they had opened my hands back up, it had taken them well over half an hour just to get my hands open. The occupational therapist's had then made splints for my hands to help keep my hands open as this would aid the recovery stage of my treatment and again I was never happy about having to wear them and would often ask members of staff if I could have a break from them as my arms would begin to ache so badly. So as the two physio;s finished the session with me they fitted all my splints, telling me in the process that I would have to get used to wearing them for longer periods of time and it would be better if I could sleep with them on too. Unknown to me at that moment whilst the physio;s were working with me my mum had arrived to see me with my stepfather as visiting time had begun for the afternoon and my mum was told to wait as they were working on me. This had sent my mum in to a panic and when the physio;s had finished she almost sprinted across the ward to see me, I said "hi mum" she immediately asked me if I was OK? I replied that "yes I'm fine", but my mum was still worried and said, "but the nurse told me they were working on you", I said "just had a physio session that's all". My mum sighed and said "oh they got me all worried I thought that something awful had happened". I could see how much my mum was worried but could now see the relief rushing over her. My mum told me that my dad would be up to see me on the Saturday as he was getting the train from London. I was looking forward to seeing my dad the last time I had seen him was in the June of that year when we had gone down to London to stay with him and his wife for a few days and take in the sights in London.

That evening my wife visited and it was so nice to be able to tell her that I was feeling so much more alert and that my breathing had stabilised, she seemed to be really struggling to come to terms with what had happened to me and me, and I remember her asking me how I could still believe in God after this. That thought had never crossed my mind and so much of that was because I could feel the love that God was pouring out upon me and see it with all of our fellow believers who were rallying around to help us, it also brought to light the verse in Job 2 again. I did my best to tell my wife that it was because I could feel Gods love and see it with my own eyes, the hour that was allotted for visiting in the evening was soon over and I had to say good-bye to my wife she told me she would be up the next day. My wife's remarks about God worried me and led me to pray for her I could see how affected she was by everything and I felt so helpless.

That night was another of being on oxygen, the ability to sleep with tubes everywhere and my splints on was not easy, I also now had to have a eye patch over my left eye as I was now unable to close my left eye so with my moon boots on and my hand splints plus a patch over my left eye I must of cut quite a sight. I also had to contend with the noise of all the machines on the ward as they bleeped through the night and was having real difficulty sleeping and just to add to that I was still being disturbed to have my breathing checked every few hours and on a number of occasions during the night I would still be awake when they came again to check my breathing. I prayed to God that I would now turn a corner with my breathing and that I would soon be sent back to ANU which compared to intensive care was ten times more comfortable an environment to be in. The great news I was now getting was that when my breathing was checked, it was now improving I was no longer getting the same result over and over again and I was so pleased, I thanked God for the healing he was already giving me. The nurse said that if I continued like this it would not be long before I would be able to leave the intensive care ward and that was like sweet music to my ears.

Malachi 4 verse 2, but for you who revere my name, the sun of righteousness will rise with healing in its wings.

I truly felt I had made my first tentative steps to recovery, I had until then been on a downward curve but finally I was seeing the first green shoots of my body fighting back. I woke that Friday morning feeling so full of the joy that God was placing in my heart and I spent much of the morning listening to the CD's that Geraldine had brought in for me, I just felt so alive, yet my body was still paralysed and I still relied upon the care of the nurses as I could not do anything for myself but I was feeling so joyous I knew that God had done something amazing.

That afternoon my consultant from ANU came to see me and I could see he was genuinely pleased with the results that he was seeing on the charts, the improvements in my breathing were quite amazing he told me, he told me that most patients with Guillain-Barre syndrome end up being ventilated when they get to the level of difficulty I had with my breathing and he felt that it was amazing that I had not had to be ventilated as he had fully expected me to have to be. He was so pleased with the progress that I had made in those few days that he told me he was happy enough for me to return to ANU and see how things went from there. I knew the reason that I had not been ventilated was because God had listened to the prayers that everyone had prayed for me and by his grace he had intervened, yes I was not fully healed but God was confounding the medical experts with how I was now starting to recover.

It was almost dinner time in the hospital when the porters arrived to take me back to the ANU ward, the nurses on ANU were so pleased to see me and many of them told me how worried they had been when I went to intensive care, it was lovely to see how much they cared and I was again reminded of how much Gods hand was at play in all that was going on. I just seemed to be surrounded by so many Christians, as I have said this ward seemed to be filled with Gods loving people and at times I felt overwhelmed by their love and care that they gave me every day.

That evening when my wife arrived it was lovely not to be on the intensive care ward and to be able to talk to her in a place where things seemed so much more relaxed even though this was still a fairly serious place to be in. It felt so wonderful to tell her that my breathing had started to improve I could see that she felt relieved that I was now out of intensive care. Ruth had brought her to see me that evening and much of the organising of who was going to bring my wife to see me and organising help at home was down to her, I was truly thankful for the love and time she was pouring out into my family. One thing that was certain was that I was going to get to know Ruth very well over the coming months as she continued to work away in supporting us as a family.

God's hand was at work in everything! Wherever I seemed to look I found God he was everywhere it humbled me so much that God loved me so much and that is the truth, God wants for all of us for us to feel his loving hand, his gentleness and his grace, his mercy but so often we fail to see it or feel it but the situation I was now in had drawn me so close to God and I was in awe of the mercy and love that I was now experiencing. The comfort that I was feeling was amazing and I knew that God was watching over me.

JOB 11 VERSE 18, And thou shalt be secure, because there is hope: yea, thou shalt dig about thee, and thou shalt take thy rest in safety.

CHAPTER 3

A NEW ANGLE OF ATTACK

Being back on ANU filled me with hope, things over the last week had been really scary but I felt really pleased to be out of intensive care. One of the patients who had been in my room when I went up to intensive had now gone home and their was now an empty bed space. Zach was still up to his antics which would still mean nights of broken sleep but it was better than being on intensive care. Just after tea time on the ward a new patient arrived and was given the bed space that was free. His first words I remember him saying as he settled in to life on the ward were, well this is a lively room any one would think that we were all ill, it made me laugh so much I knew straight away that I was going to get on with my new room mate. His name was Barry and we had soon become good mates, we would often pass the hours just telling each other jokes and basically poking fun at each other. Being in a hospital is often the very place that a good sense of humour is truly a key element, it is so amazing what laughter can do when everything is not so rosy health wise, I know that it helped me through the day to day life on the ward.

That Saturday my dad visited me as planned and it was so good to see him he told me how his church in London had been praying for me and that my aunt's church in Scotland had been holding me in prayer too. The news that so many people were holding me in prayer left me feeling overwhelmed with just how much love was being poured out for me, God's grace was just flowing out and yet again I felt so blessed it was just staggering to know how much people cared. My dad was travelling back to London the next morning but he told me that if there was anything he could do all I had to do was ask, the truth was that I felt everyone was already doing more than I could imagine but I told him that if I thought of anything I would let him know. When the afternoon visiting hours were over my dad told me he was going to stay around for the evening visiting as well and told me he was off to find the hospital canteen.

That evening my dad reappeared from his time in the canteen and very shortly afterwards my wife arrived, it was lovely just to have a normal chat together that evening. So often when visitors came to see you everything just seemed to revolve around the illness I had and sure it did have its very own novelty factor with it being so rare. My dad asked lots of questions about my illness but in all honesty even I did not know that much about it. Having time with family and friends was always very special but the time always seemed to fly by and before I knew it I was saying my goodbye's. I thanked my dad for coming to see me and he told me that he would try to get back up soon, Saying goodbye to the people you love after such a short time with them was something I always found very hard and I always felt that it was the hardest part of being ill.

My body over that next week showed little improvement if any at all but my health remained stable, the physio;s were now trying new things with me and were now trying to get me sat up even if it was only for about two minutes, it was taking the work of four physio;s just to get me sat up from a lying position the amount of effort for just two minutes seemed somehow criminal but they informed me that it was essential that they began to start trying to work on my core muscles as it might just wake them up from their slumber, it was strange having to be propped up by one of the physio;s from behind and the sessions with the physio;s were really tiring and took so much out of me that I would end up needing a sleep right after a session with them In their gym. The amount of energy something so simple now took seemed unbelievable.

On the weekend that my dad had visited me I also met Barry's wife Lisa and she took pity on me from the beginning, she would so often come over and give me a drink holding my cup of water for me while I sucked on a straw, but even better than that Lisa came with goodies for Barry (chocolate) and would always offer me a piece, I felt awkward about taking Barry's treats but Lisa just told me that he had enough of his own so I was not to worry. The chocolate she brought for Barry was caramac I have to say I had not had caramac since being in my teens and right away realised what I had been missing all these years, Barry joked with his wife about the fact that she was hand feeding me his chocolate and their was a real sense of good humour between us all.

There was never a dull moment in that room, there were so many moments of laughter but we also had moments of real worry we had all taken a bad turn at some point or other but praise God that we had all did pull through those scary moments.

On the Wednesday of the following week when my wife came to see me she asked me if it would be all right for her to take our son to Blackpool on the Friday evening as there was a coach trip on and all the rides at the fair were open late, she thought it would be a good idea just to give him a night away from home and to have some fun. It did not take much thinking about really my poor boy had been through so much with me being ill so to give him a night where he could have some fun sounded great to me. A friend of ours had agreed to go with my wife anyway with her son so it was not as if she was going to be alone. My wife told me that she would come to see me on the Saturday evening and she thanked me for letting her take him.

On that Friday evening my catheter was removed as I was experiencing problems with it and I was in so much pain, it was yet another step forward for me, it was such a small step to take but to me it felt as though it was a huge step I felt that healing process was truly beginning.

I spent much of that evening thinking about my family, all out in Blackpool having fun I felt so sad that I was not there with them. It really did make me feel as though I was missing out. Saturday came and went by and the evening visiting hours were already almost over and there was still no sign of my wife and I lay there worrying about her, it was not like her not to come. As I lay there wondering why she was so late one of the nurses came in to see me she had just gotten off the phone and it was my wife who had rung the ward, I was so relieved to hear that she was fine but had not been able to get up to the hospital as the lift had not turned up to bring her to see me. I was sad that she could not make it, I was not too worried though these sorts of things do happen from time to time anyway, I was just sad as I had looked forward to seeing her and everybody in church was already doing more than I could imagine and I was sure that one more day would not harm me.

Sunday afternoon my mum visited me, she told me that she was worried about my wife as she had spoken to her on the phone and my wife had seemed very uneasy while they were talking. My wife had told my mum that she had something that she needed to talk through with me but she would not tell my mum what it was. My Mum then asked me if I had any idea what it was that my wife would want to talk to me about and if I knew if there was anything that was troubling her? if my wife did have anything that was troubling her I certainly did not know what it was. It did seem odd to me that my wife had not mentioned anything to me, but the stress of the last couple of weeks was probably enough of a worry all in itself and so I was not surprised if she was uneasy and needed to talk to me. My mum about an hour into the visiting time told me she had to go and began to put her coat on, just as she and my stepfather were about to leave my wife arrived with two of our friends from church Ruth and Michelle. My mum glanced around at me as she left with a frown on her face, I knew that deep down she wanted to stay and see what my wife needed to talk to me about but Ruth and Michelle had walked off with her chatting to her and my stepfather.

My wife came up to my bed and held my hand and she was shaking I could not put my finger on why she was so nervous and I asked her if Ruth and Michelle were coming in too. She replied that they would be in a minute but that she had something to tell me first. she began to cry and just kept repeating that she was sorry, I had no idea what she was sorry for and so I asked her? My wife hung her head and then told me that she had cheated on me on the Friday night with an old flame who had also gone on the trip to Blackpool. I lay there feeling completely stunned for a few moments, She told me it had been a moment of complete weakness and that she had felt awful about it straight after she had done it and told me that it would never happen again and asked me if I could forgive her for what she had done?

I felt as though I had been mortally wounded and I lay there unable to get my head around what my wife had just told me. Nothing of what she had said made any sense to me at all, but Acts 5 verse 31 came to mind though, God exalted him to his right own hand as prince and saviour that he might give repentance and forgiveness of sins. God himself could forgive us of all our sins, all we have to do is repent of them and ask for Gods forgiveness I lay there and asked myself who was I to refuse to forgive my wife for what she had done. When our father in heaven can forgive us our sins to the point where he does not even remember them, I truly felt that I had no right to lie there in my hospital bed and to tell my wife that I did not forgive her even though I knew how hard it would be to say those words.

So with tears welling in my eyes I told her that I forgave her for what she had done, it was now her turn to look stunned and she asked me how I could? She looked totally bemused that I could forgive her, I answered her that it was because I loved her so deeply and that God can forgive each of us for our sins. My wife leant forward and kissed me and thanked me, there was still a look of total bemusement on her face but she looked totally relieved. She thanked me again for forgiving her and then went to get Ruth and Michelle who had waited near the ward entrance for my wife to come and get them when she had finished talking to me! Ruth and Michelle came back in with my wife and Ruth said to me "bless you Jez that was a tough thing to do". Visiting time was already nearly over and my wife told me how she was going to put everything into our marriage to make it up to me and told me how much she loved me before she had to go.

That night I felt so empty the illness had taken a toll on my body but had not left me feeling defeated if anything my resolve to overcome my illness had never been stronger, but this had come like a hammer blow to my chest. It was worse that any physical pain and that night when the lights went off I cried as quietly as I could in my bed, I still could not wipe the tears from my eyes and my eyes stung as I wept quietly. The next few days passed in what I can only describe as a blur, my wife visited me each day along with friends from church, my elder brother Paul popped in after work on the Wednesday afternoon as well as my mum and stepfather David. I was not ready to tell my mum what my wife had done and ended up concocting a story just to appease her although I doubted that she truly believed the story I told her, but there was no way I was ready to reveal the awful truth of what had actually happened. I truly felt as though I was at the centre of a storm and that I was clinging on for dear life, My wife most days she visited me would ask me how I could forgive her for what she had done as she herself could not forgive herself for it. The truth was during those few weeks after, I was just so numb from all the pain that in truth it was just a question that I wished would go away. I would answer my wife with the words that she was already forgiven and I kept on telling her that she had my forgiveness and it was time to move on.

Physically my body was still showing little progress as I was yet to see any signs of movement return to any of my limbs. In physio sessions

I continued with sitting up exercises, trying to get my core muscles to switch back on. During my third week in hospital they decided that it would be a good idea to start getting me sat in a chair for a short while on the ward. They had found a suitable chair that was adjustable in height and in posture position and had wheeled it through to their gym. One of the new contraptions I was going to get very acquainted with was the hoist machine. After the Physio;s had gotten me in the chair with the hoist, James the head Physio asked me if I felt comfortable I answered him that I felt fine for the moment! The physio;s were all excited about wheeling me back onto the ward and said "just you wait and see what reaction you get when the staff see you sat in a chair"! One of the physio;s took my bed back onto the ward and then came back to help James bring me back from the gym.

I said earlier that I felt like Frankenstein when I was on intensive care, now being wheeled around in a chair back onto the ward I felt like Davros the leader of the Daleks from Dr who! The staff were so upbeat about seeing me sat in a chair and Barry my fellow compatriot said "hey look at you looking like the king of the ward sat there on your throne". Truthfully I wanted to give a royal wave as I was wheeled back into my bed space but I had to make do with a nod of my head instead. The physio;s told me that they were briefing the staff over how long to leave me in the chair as it was probably going to be very tiring for me, to begin with they set a time limit in the chair at half an hour. My physio session finished around two that afternoon and I had only been sat there a few minutes on the ward when visiting time began. Lisa, Barry's wife was really impressed to see me sat up and out of my bed as all the other times she had been I had always been lying down so she was suitably impressed. I was not expecting any visitors that afternoon but around half an hour later I had surprise visitors, John and Sharon! They had left our church and moved to the south coast earlier in the year, I know that moving away had been a really difficult thing for them to do and I was truly so pleased to see them. It was lovely to spend time with them asking them how they were and how their children were getting on, they in turn asked me how I was and it really touched me that they came to see me and yet again I was left just feeling so blessed by the love being poured out by everybody. Seeing friends always brought a smile to my face.

I was unfortunately beginning to wane fast in the chair and was really beginning to feel a lot of pain just from being in a sitting position John and Sharon could see that I was in pain and asked me if I needed a nurse. I told them that I had already been in my chair for thirty minutes and it was now getting too much for me. So Sharon went to get the nurses to come and put me back in my bed. Before they left they told me that I was in their prayers and I was so thankful to hear that. The nurses clipped my harness onto the hoist machine and then lifted me out of the chair and back into my bed, the sheer relief as my weight was taken by the harness in stead of the chair! I ached so badly, I had in fact been in the chair more like forty minutes by the time I was lifted back into bed and it seemed so amazing how badly my body coped with just sitting in a chair.

In every day life it is something we just do not think about, it is a natural part of our daily lives to sit down and stand up and feel comfortable while we are sat, so to have a body that struggles to cope with just half an hour felt so alien to how it should feel. Having been a lorry driver for eight years I was used to being sat for long periods of time whilst at the wheel of the lorry I drove each day. At times I felt like a prisoner in an alien body and what made that worse was the very fact that I could feel everything but not move at all. Being paralysed from the neck down was an eye opener in to a very different world and I found myself totally able to sympathise with anyone who was like I was only permanently! Being able to do nothing for yourself yet know how to do the very things that all the care staff were doing for you every day was totally frustrating. God however as I have already stated was with me the whole time and the one thing I felt he was teaching me was patience, patience was not one of my strong points, I would so often just hurl myself head first into any project before truly thinking about what I was doing. Without God and his peace and the love being daily poured out for me I do not know how I would and could have held on through the storm, yet I found that he was giving me such inner strength to get through everything that was going on.

My wife over that next few weeks seemed to be coping better than she had and she finally came to a place where she was able to thank me for forgiving her for her adultery, it was so nice to hear those words from her as I had wondered if she had wanted me to forgive her as her response had seemed as though she was shocked that I could forgive her. She told me that she really wanted to put things right and start afresh in our marriage, I was so pleased to hear this forgiving her had been the hardest thing I had ever had to do. The pain I felt when she told me of her adultery was immense and continued to eat at me some days while I lay there in my hospital bed still unable to move. I tried so hard to forget about it but every time I thought about my wife the thoughts of what she had done would race through my mind. I loved her so much and we had two beautiful children and so to hear her tell me she was truly sorry and wanted to do everything she could to sort out the mess just meant so much to me. I felt that all was not lost and I thanked God yet again that he had given me the courage to forgive her for what she had done.

1 Thessalonians 5 verse 18

In every thing give thanks: for this is the will of God in Christ Jesus concerning you.

October was almost over and I had now spent over four weeks in the care of the NHS, I still could not move any of my limbs but on the plus side my face was beginning to return to normal and I was no longer needing an eye patch over my left eye as I could now close it again. During that fourth week I had met a new consultant who was going to be taking over my care once I was moved to the rehabilitation ward at the hospital. She had told me that she was also a consultant within a hospital in Stockport that was also a rehabilitation hospital. She explained that she felt that I would really benefit from going there and it was closer to home for my wife, family and friends to be able to visit me. There was for the moment still a number of hurdles that I needed to get over before she could begin to look at moving me there, but she seemed genuinely pleased with the progress that I appeared to be making for the moment. She told me that once I was moved off the ANU ward and onto the rehabilitation ward known as C2 that she would then look to get me transferred to this hospital in Stockport.

It was so pleasing to hear what was in store for me once I was well enough and it give me more encouragement and faith to keep on trusting God. Also on that fourth week I was given a really big surprise by the staff as a special treat had been set up for me one afternoon, they got me ready and hoisted me into a wheelchair and they then wheeled me out of my room and into a visiting room where I found my wife and my children waiting for me along with Jane who is a parish nurse who had brought them to see me. It was the first time I had seen my children since falling ill and seeing them almost brought tears to my eyes, I had missed them so much and it was so wonderful to see them.

My son was really shocked to see his dad in a wheelchair and seemed really upset at seeing his dad so ill, I really felt for him and wanted him to come over and give me a cuddle but it was something he was not ready to do at that time. My Daughter just stared at me intently, it was like she was inspecting every detail of my face just to be sure it actually was me. Goodness only knows what she thought, she was only just over six months old but I could tell from the way she was looking at me that she recognised me, I had lay there in my hospital bed worrying that she would not know who I was.

That half an hour that I had with my children was just so special. I had met Jane a few times before as she and her husband Peter both went to the Anglican church on the estate where I lived, I thanked her for bringing them to see me and she told me that it had been a pleasure and was all part of her parish nursing, but I was so overwhelmed by the love and sheer support that everybody was giving me and family and it truly touched my heart so much.

Friends from church and from all over the UK were still holding me in prayer many of those who were praying I did not know but it always touched my heart when people told me that they had prayed for me. The level of prayer going on for me was just phenomenal and once again I felt those prayers as my body showed a little more improvement. My breathing was beginning to show slow but steady progress and my core muscles had improved in physio sessions as I was now sitting for slightly longer than I had been when I had first begun the sessions with them. By the end of October the doctors were much happier and a decision was made that I was now well enough to be transferred onto the rehabilitation ward at the hospital. Barry was still not well enough to come off ANU and I was sad to be leaving my new friend behind. On the day I was moved to C2 his wife took down my home address and telephone number and in turn they gave me their contact details. Although I was sad to be moving on I was also pleased as it meant that I was now on the mend, very slowly but I was heading in the right direction.

C2 as it turned out was two floors up within the same building so it was not much of a move and I was soon settling into my new environment, the ward was a mirror image of ANU and I even ended up with the window bed space again not that I could see anything I was now three floors up from the ground level, but I did have a great view of the sky. One thing that struck me straight away was that it no longer felt like I was living in a tropical forest so I was really thankful for that. I was looking forward to being able to hopefully get a full nights rest, Zach's night time antics had kept me awake as much as the pain I was often in. How wrong was I though I was now sharing a room with yet another man who seemed to find it entertaining to wake half the ward up in the middle of the night shouting at nurses, I felt sorry for him though as he was always so confused and would often ask me what time it was and after I had told him he would say, thanks and then go on to tell me that he would have to get ready for work soon. I forget how many times I had to tell him that he was in hospital. Being moved on to the rehabilitation ward proved to be a big turning point for me, I knew that God had saved me. It seems strange to say it now but I knew that I was never going to work as a lorry driver again, in my prayers every night I thanked God for saving me and asked that he show me what it was that I would do in the future. I knew that God had saved me so that people could see Gods work, and hear how amazing Gods healing is, John 9 verse 3, neither hath this man sinned nor his parents: but that the works of God should be manifest in him.

Many friends who came to see me told me what strength and encouragement I gave them with the way that I was facing my illness and I personally found it hard to see how I was an encouragement, I could feel God giving me the strength for each day and night that I was in hospital. I also felt that complaining to God about what had happened would do me no good, no the Lord had given me a cross to carry and all I could do was trust him and take up the challenges put before me. A couple of days into my stay on C2 the man who was in the next bed to me was told that he could go home so we were down to just three of us in the room. The next day the nurses came in and began preparing the bed for a new patient, I watched as they worked away making the bed up and then as one of them wrote the new patients name above the bed space, Barry! The thought struck me that it might be my mate from ANU and so I asked the nurse what ward he was coming from and sure enough it was ANU, I laughed out loud knowing that we were once again going to be together in the same room.

When he arrived with his wife Lisa that afternoon we all laughed, I jokingly asked him if he was following me, but oh boy the great or as it probably was the not so great comedy duo were back together. I was really glad to have Barry next to me on the ward and an extra plus was that Lisa was so caring and always made sure that I had a drink or a bite of chocolate. The nurses on C2 soon got to realise that together we were the ward clowns and spent a good portion of the day laughing and joking.

One thing that I never looked forward to having done was having my blood taken and it was nearly a daily experience for me during my time at Hope hospital, one of the nurses on ANU had very early on in my stay at Hope hospital commented that I looked like Ryan Giggs the footballer of Manchester United and from that moment on at the hospital I was known as Giggsy by most of the staff.

I found it quite amusing to be called Giggsy and one of the male nurses who regularly came to take my blood would always come into the room I was in and say to me, morning Giggsy how are you' and often I would reply jokingly, well since I've been paralysed I have not scored many goals! It was always good friendly banter and often just took me away from the precarious way things were with my health. Remaining positive when faced with such trials is so important. I saw many a patient who on receiving bad results or just struggling with their particular illness would just throw in the towel and give up and I always felt so sad when they did, it was never nice to see someone just wallow in their own self pity and give up.

My time in hospital did give me plenty of time for prayer and to spend time with God. Every night before going to sleep I would pray for the other patients around me and thank God for his mercy and for the love and caring support that he was wrapping around me and my family, my life before I had been ill was always so busy that although I did pray to God I never felt really close to him, but today I thank God because if I had never gone through the trauma that I did I would not be the person I am today and know his love so well and be walking so closely with him.

As November began I could feel that there was a sadness about my wife, she never looked happy and she would sometimes arrive to see me and be very angry. She felt that people were interfering in our marriage, members of my family were mentioned as well as some of our friends. I found it hard to deal with the level of verbal abuse coming from her. I felt as though I was under yet another form of attack and it was always me that was on the end of an ear bashing from her. Every day before my wife came to see me I would be apprehensive about her visit as I never knew what mood she was likely to be in though I was now slowly recovering I still felt as though I was in the middle of a storm. It was always so difficult to take as all I could see was how much everyone was rallying around us, they were uniting and pouring out their love upon us as a family, so many times I had to calm my wife down when she arrived to see me as the anger poured out from her mouth. The way she was talking about family and friends alike made me dread her visits. I cannot say that I looked forward to seeing her whilst she threw these crazy accusations around that everyone was against her and was judging her, many of the people she was angry with did not even know what she had done anyway as I had kept it that way.

In physio sessions they were now strapping me to a new contraption called a tilt table, the physio;s told me that they were going to use this machine to get me used to being stood up again, so I was transferred across onto it and then straps were put across my legs chests and arms so that I would not fall off. Once they had me fastened down the head physio told me that she was going to gradually move me into an upright position. She would tilt me so far and then ask me if I was OK? The first few degrees that I was left on were fine so she asked me if I was up for trying to see if they could get me into an almost upright position? I was fine with trying it, the physio;s had told me that most patients who have spent as long as I had lying down often ended up feeling very faint as the blood rushes down your body into your legs. Finally I was almost in a stood up position and it amazed me to be looking down upon the staff as I had gotten used to looking up at them, the head physio asked me if I felt OK and at the moment she asked the question I did feel fine, but just a few moments later I began to feel really dizzy and sweat began pouring down my neck I told the physio;s that I was feeling really weird and they then rushed to get me lying down again. As the table began to right itself I could feel myself blacking out, it scared me that something so simple had made me feel so unwell. The table finally got to the middle position and for a few moments I lay there feeling completely dazed and worn out. They quickly got a heart monitor on me and gave me some oxygen and after a few minutes my blood pressure stabilised and I began to come round properly. Once I was settled and back in my bed they took me back onto the ward.

I was totally exhausted from the session with them and needed to get some sleep but I was aware of the nurses checking on me a little more regularly for the rest of that day. The whole episode with the tilt table had made me feel very wary of going on it again when I had my next session of physio. The physio;s told me that we had to keep on going with more of the same so again a few days later I was strapped to the tilt table for another session. I lay there expecting it to be as bad as the first time, but this time I felt no ill effects while I was put through the varying degree's the table put me in. As a precaution this time the physio;s had put a blood pressure strap on my arm before we started the therapy. I was so pleased that I did not end up feeling faint this time around and the physio;s were equally pleased too as I had scared them a little the last time too. Again I felt as though I had made a small break through in my recovery and even though it was such a small thing that we were doing as I was still unable to move any part of my body it gave me such strength to keep on fighting as much as I could to recover.

I had now spent eight weeks in hospital and time had simply flown by, my consultant came to see me and told me that as soon as they had a bed space over at the Devonshire unit in Stockport she was going to get me transferred over there to continue my rehabilitation, the Devonshire unit was a specialised unit that helped patients with the recovery side of neurological conditions. Guillain-Barre was such a strange illness to suffer with, knowing that effectively my brain was what was at fault for the illness as it had kept on sending signals to my immune system to fight against a virus when the virus had already been effectively dealt with by my immune system was just crazy, somehow my brains circuitry had gotten itself into a right mess and had cross wired itself, or that was how I viewed it anyway. Being paralysed was really hard to deal with I had not yet seen any signs of physical recovery but God had taken me to a place where I knew I had to just trust him. His love was flowing into my life and he was giving me such courage to keep on fighting when everything seemed to be stacked against me.

As the end of November approached I began to see the first signs of physical recovery in my body. One afternoon I lay there in my hospital bed trying to move at least some part of my seemingly lifeless body, it was something that every day since being in hospital I had tried to do but as of yet I had seen no results from my efforts. However this particular day l managed to wiggle my fingers a little on my left hand, I stared at my hand in amazement and watched as just the slightest movement could be seen! I now needed a second opinion and called Barry over to have a look. Barry came across to my bed and he and I watched my left hand as I tried to move my fingers and sure enough Barry also saw them wiggle just the slightest bit. Barry was so pleased for me and told me "that's great mate you will soon be running around". A short while later one of the nurses came into the room and I showed her what I was now able to do, she was really pleased for me and told me that she would have to put it into my notes. Every visitor I got from that moment on was subjected to the same show, I was sure some people needed super strength glasses just to be able to see the microscopic movements I was now able to perform but I was so elated just to be able to move them, I knew now that the physical healing had truly begun in my body and I praised God for that.

I moved hospitals during the last week of November but before that move took place the movement in the fingers of my left hand had now progressed to the point where I could move my left arm and lift it very slightly off the mattress of my bed. I was so encouraged as the ability to move my arm had spread so fast and I was feeling stronger every day. My right arm had also begun to show the same recovery and I was now at least able to move both arms a little, Gods amazing healing was now in full flow. Hebrews 12 verses 12 & 13: Therefore strengthen your feeble arms and weak knee's, so that the lame may not be disabled but rather healed.

I was so happy that God was now healing my body but I truly believed that I had to meet God half way, which meant me putting one hundred percent effort into my recovery. I knew that I had to have total faith in God and I trusted him so much, before I was ill I would not let go and I had to be in control and would not let God in. But now God had taught me that I could trust him and put my life totally in his care, it sounds strange but I knew that God had had to take me to a place where I could not do anything for myself so that I would fully trust him in any situation I found myself in. Over those initial weeks in hospital my faith and trust in God had grown immensely, the Holy spirit had been with me all the time I had been ill. I felt as though Jesus had been sat next to my bed caring for me every day and night. Jesus had been with me through all the pain and suffering but for me the most wonderful thing he was doing was the work he was doing in my heart and soul and I was now looking forward to wherever Jesus was going to take me next. In Jeremiah 18 we read about a pot that is marred and the potter is shaping it into a new pot, shaping it as seemed best to him. I felt that God was now doing that with me, the old me that was all too easily swayed by money or of things of the world was being broken, God was at the potters wheel shaping me into a new man and I embraced the changes he was doing with me.

Moving hospital was both a wonderful thing to do and sad because of having to say goodbye to Barry for the second time, but knowing that I was moving on to the major recovery stage for my illness gave me great encouragement. I was glad that Barry's wife Lisa had also been there when I left Hope hospital as I had gotten to know them both so well over the weeks we had shared a room on the two wards we had inhabited, but now ahead for me lay an ambulance ride across Manchester from Salford all the way to Stockport. I was glad to be moving nearer to home as it now meant that my children could visit me and the hospital was only a bus ride away for my wife so if she wanted to visit it was now going to be so much easier for her. I felt so alive I had been surrounded by darkness and suffering on a scale that I had never encountered before, yet Jesus had been with me all the way comforting me and giving me strength to keep on fighting and his love was pouring into my life. I lay there in the ambulance on my way to Stockport feeling so loved by God and so encouraged that I was now starting to get better.

CHAPTER 4

MORE GRIEF

I arrived at the Devonshire unit in Stockport and the set up there was very different from Hope hospital instead of five man rooms most of the rooms here were two man rooms, but even more surprising for me was the fact that I was going to be on my own in this room to begin with as they had no other new male patients due to be admitted. It was a big change from Hope hospital and it felt a lot more homely, one of the health care assistants who helped me settle in was called Bob. Bob as it turned out was a former fireman and soldier, so having spent six years in the armed forces myself we got on straight away.

When I was leaving Hope hospital I had asked one of the nurses to ring my family to tell them that I was being transferred that afternoon to Stockport, the message had gotten through and my mum soon arrived along with my stepfather David, Bob told me that he would see if their was a spare wheelchair that I could use. I lay there a few moments checking out my new surroundings before he returned with a red wheelchair, he explained that by rights it did belong to another patient but that the patient no longer used it. He got me harnessed up and then hoisted me out of my bed and into the wheelchair.

He then wheeled me around to the main foyer of the building where my mum and stepfather were waiting to see me. I just had time to say hello to my mum and stepfather when I saw my wife approaching the main doors, my daughter was with her in her pram fast asleep but my wife seemed agitated and something was clearly bothering her. When one of the nurses came past us as we were chatting my wife asked her if it was

OK for her to take me for a trip around the grounds of the hospital. The nurse replied that it was fine but she would have to put a blanket over me, so the nurse went and got a blanket to wrap around my legs and waist. My wife asked my mum if she could take me alone and asked my mum and stepfather if they would watch our daughter while we went for a quick spin around the grounds and my mum said that was fine.

My wife opened the door of the ward and the cold of the outside November weather hit me straight away, she wheeled me up the side of one of the adjacent buildings and around a corner. Something seemed to be really eating at her, to begin with she just asked me how I was feeling and in general chit chat she said to me "you must be pleased to be a bit closer to home"? Which I of course I was, we were soon out of sight of the Devonshire unit and around the corner of the building we had just walked up the side of. Now the real questions began, my wife began with, "do you really love me"? it was said so coldly! I answered her, "yes that's why I forgave you" but she was quick to snap back barely giving my answer chance to be finished, "well have you ever cheated on me"? This was not just some lovely walk me and my wife were taking around the grounds of the hospital.

She had wanted to be alone with me so that she could interrogate me, the question of me being unfaithful to her took me completely off guard. I had just spent the last two months in hospital fighting for my life! I replied quickly, "No never" my wife again barely gave time for my answer before she continued on with her interrogation, "you must have been" she said coldly, "you were desperate to take your old job back delivering to all those hotels to all those women!" It was not so much a question but a statement of how she felt about the work I did and in her reasoning my only reason for taking my old job back was that I was jumping into bed with women at the hotels. I truly could not believe what I was hearing, I was now being accused of the very thing that I had had the grace to forgive her for. God had blessed me with that job as the job I had had just did not suit me and I would often go into work dreading the day ahead, no the only reason I had jumped at the offer of work from my old boss was that I truly enjoyed the work and overtime was always available to bump up your weekly wage and I had always been a firm believer in supporting my family so I had always worked hard to provide for them. Again I answered my wife's accusations with a "No never! I have never done that" my answer did not seem to appease her and she just said "whatever then".

My wife seemed bitterly frustrated with me and very angry, it was as if she had wanted me to have been jumping into bed with other women while I was out working, and I was not giving her what she wanted in her minds view of things. We finally rounded the last corner of our walk around the grounds, and the Devonshire unit was back in sight just then my wife leaned in closer to me and dealt me another huge blow. "Well I have done it again Jez" she said, "I have cheated on you again" it was practically all she said to me and their was no sorry this time from her and the way she said it it was as if she was just reading out a news broadcast. I got no apology and not even a hint of remorse in her voice, I was completely blown away. The whole journey around the grounds had been one body blow after another, nothing in that moment made any sense to me, she had always professed her love to me and told me daily that she loved me very deeply and had always said that she would never hurt me. I loved her so much that a train travelling at seventy miles an hour could not have hurt me as much as she had just done. I was glad when we finally arrived back at my new ward. My mum I knew could sense that something had gone on and she asked me if I was OK, I was in no state of mind to be answering questions so I just told her that I was fine.

I was so glad when visiting time had finished and I could be alone for a while, a few hours earlier I had looked upon the move to this new hospital as a huge step forward not only for my physical recovery, but also as I was now closer to home that it would also be a huge step forward for me and my wife to start piecing back together our marriage after all that had happened. My wife's adultery had been a huge shock to me, and I knew that my wife always felt a huge amount of guilt over what she had done but right at that moment I was numb with the pain of being hurt again. Bob got me hoisted back into bed and I lay there in bed quietly pondering the new bombshell my wife had just given me. The pain of dealing with an illness was enough in itself without having to deal with all this turmoil in my marriage as well and now it seemed as though my wife did not care any more, it was as though she had had enough of me. It really hurt that she was not even sorry for what she had done this time, the pain of what she had just told me was so overwhelming and it was so much worse than the physical pain that I endured every day and there were days when I was in excruciating pain.

I did not feel at that moment that I could talk to anyone about what my wife had just told me so I cried out to God. I asked God why this was happening as in my suffering I myself could not make any sense of it, tears often flowed down my cheeks once I had settled down for the night, once the lights were out in my hospital room, I thanked God that I at least was on my own in that room and no one else had to endure my suffering as well as their own. Crying out to God in this way reminded me of Job and how he could not understand why he was suffering as he was, I had felt that moving hospitals was a positive thing but after what had just happened I felt as though the storm surrounding me was growing ever stronger.

Despite how awful things were right at that moment God was there with me giving me strength to get through each day, his grace he was giving me and I needed it so much. The pain I was in through how my wife was treating me was overwhelming me at times.

Psalm 119 verse 50, My comfort in my suffering is this: Your promise preserves my life.

My wife visited me again on the Saturday with my son and my daughter, I still did not know what to say to her or how to approach the issues that we had going on, so I immersed myself in my children, enjoying the time I had with them that afternoon. I had missed them both so terribly and longed to hold them both and give them a cuddle, my son was now more willing to come over and cuddle me than he had been the first time he was allowed to see me when I was in Hope hospital. My wife brought my daughter up to my bed and put her in my lap so I could cuddle her, it was such a special moment I felt as though I had missed so much of her development over the last few months and she had grown so much in that short time. Sadly my body was not up to holding my daughter for very long as fatigue and pain would leave me feeling very uncomfortable very quickly and after what must have been only just over a minute I had to ask my wife to pick her up as the pain became to unbearable.

My daughter was only just over eight months old and probably only just weighed over a stone but even that was too much for me, I so wanted those moments to become something that I could do regularly and it truly spurred me on to work hard at getting stronger so that I could again be a father to my children. My wife had caught the bus up to the hospital that Saturday afternoon and the time with them just flew by and they soon had to go, I thanked her for coming to see me and told them all that I loved them very much.

My wife even gave me a kiss before she went but I could sense the turmoil in her heart. I still did not know what to say, to every answer I did her give she always had another angle that seemed to destroy any hope that we could salvage our marriage. My every thought was about how I could effectively turn around the mess that our marriage was in, but other than me being at home permanently so that I could spend time with my wife to try and heal our marriage and our love for one another I did not know what to do. Ruth visited me on the Sunday evening and when I told her what my wife had said the day I arrived in Stockport it turned out that my wife had already confided in Ruth about it but not told her that she was going to interrogate me over the same thing. Ruth told me that she was going to be spending a lot more time with my wife and had suggested counselling for her, she also explained everything that she and our friends were doing for my wife while I was ill and So much was being done by everybody. work party's had been put in place to help clean our home for my wife and all sorts of general help from our friends was going on every week.

Ruth was putting such a lot in to helping us sort out the mess where I could not, and it really soothed me to know that not only was she putting so much in but that everybody was. Not being able to do anything myself was totally frustrating, but knowing that love and time was being so graciously poured in to my family left me marvelling at the love God has for every one of us. Our friends did not have to do all that they were doing yet they poured out that love every day for us. As December rushed by I physically made very slow progress, I was still in need of as much care as I had needed when I was fully immobile, but my arms were coming on very well and I was now rather haphazardly able to turn pages in books with my hands. The only downside being that occasionally I ended up ripping pages straight out of the books or magazines that I read. One thing that was hampering me however was that I had to do a lot of squinting as my glasses were at home so I asked my wife to bring them in for me, but just to add insult to injury on the night she did bring them to hospital one of the lenses popped right out of the frame. Ruth had brought my wife to see me on that particular evening and she told me that she would take them to her opticians to have them mended for me, I was so thankful to her. Ruth asked me if their was anything else that I needed? In all my time in hospital I had not had a bible and had had to rely upon my memory or friends to open their bible's when they came to see me, Ruth jotted down my request and said that she was sure that she had an old good news bible at home somewhere that I could use.

About a week later Ruth came to see me on her way home from work, I had not been expecting any visitors that evening when she came so I was really pleased to see her and she came bearing gifts. she had in hand my repaired Glasses, I tried them on and was surprised at how clean the lenses were it was like they were brand new again, I thanked her for having them fixed for me but she told me that it was a pleasure she then told me that she had another little something for me and out of her bag she pulled an old good news bible, Ruth apologised over the fact that it was only a good news bible but I was ecstatic about it.

Having had to rely upon just my memory for the last few months had been really hard but now I could truly get stuck into reading the word of God and I certainly did have plenty of time on my hands to do so. Ruth went on to tell me that this particular bible had been one of her daughters bibles and that it did not matter if I ripped the odd page out of it while I was turning pages in my rather haphazard way, before she left that evening Ruth sat and prayed with me. She had been deeply involved with all that was happening from the onset of my illness and her prayers reflected that as she prayed for my physical healing but also for the emotional healing needed for both me and my wife over the state of our marriage. Being able to read properly again was so wonderful, putting my glasses on my self was quite an operation for me, I still could not lift my arms high enough to be able to hook the arms of my glasses over my ears so it was down to an old army saying of improvise, adapt, and overcome. So after a few minutes of trying to work out what to do I finally fell upon what I thought should be the solution for this problem, I opened the arms of my glasses whilst still in the case and then putting the case on the table in front of me and then leaned my head downwards to my table hoping to slide the glasses over my ears in the process. I will be quite honest and say it did not work straight away and took several attempts before I finally did manage to get them on but eventually I had success. Being able to read again without having to squint was a wonderful feeling and I got stuck into the bible that Ruth had brought me. It felt so good to be able to read the word of God again and no longer have to rely upon my memory, it was like having an old friend back and I felt so blessed reading scripture after so long without it.

Having moved hospital meant having new physio and occupational therapists, and on my first Monday in the hospital I was put through an examination by the physio department and met the occupational therapist's. The physio examination took about an hour as they checked for strength all over my body, they used a chart where 5 was very good and 1-2 very weak. It was no surprise to me that I scored in the 1-2 zone all over my body, Mark the head physio on the unit told me that my physio sessions would be very frequent at least twice a day. He looked genuinely excited to be able to work with a patient with severe weakness. He told me that most of the time with patients it tends to be certain areas of the body that they target but with me he would get to work on every muscle group in the body.

In occupational therapy sessions much of the work at this early stage of my recovery was centred around getting my hands to work better, I had found out in that first week there that I could just about write my name, only now left handed! My right hand was not strong enough to hold a pen yet and I could not lift it far enough off a table to be of any use anyway. So I went to town on using my left hand, Having pre illness been right handed! Learning to use my left hand to write at first was really hard to do, but over the months of my rehabilitation I found that my left hand was by far the better when it came to writing so I have remained left handed. Having had the examinations it was now down to the hard work of trying to rehabilitate my severely weak body and I was determined to meet the challenge head on, God had given me his strength and I was determined to use that.

My stepfather in mid December had asked to see me, he explained that there were some financial problems that had arisen and he needed to speak to me, my mum and my church pastor Jim came along to the meeting as well. The room I was in I was now sharing with a lovely guy who was also called Barry and even stranger than that, when I was moved to Stockport he had gone in to the bed space I had vacated in Salford so it turned out that we both knew Barry and Lisa, it is a small world.

The things that David my stepfather wanted to discuss were of a sensitive financial nature so I asked the nursing staff if they could partition part of the dining room off for us so we could talk and the staff were more than happy to help. They arrived around two in the afternoon that Tuesday in December and we made our way down the hospital corridor to the area the nurses had partitioned off for us, David had a file in hand and to my horror it was filled with unpaid bills, the list of bills that were not getting paid was very extensive some of which my wife had promised me she was paying. I did not doubt for a minute that things had been tough for her while I was ill but the amount that we owed was astronomical. Admittedly some of the bills were from my bank account and she had no access to my account to pay them, but what disturbed me the most was that some of the bills that were in complete disarray I had in the beginning of October straightened out for her, my wife had never been fantastic with money but I had always stressed the need to keep up with our bills. I had managed to straighten out debts that she had had over the years we had been together, But now again bills were in complete disarray, all the debts combined amounted up to just over a thousand pounds and all this in the space of a couple of months, I was so annoyed that my wife had allowed us to get in to a complete nightmare of a mess financially again. The worst thing was that at every moment over the last few months my wife could have turned to my family or the church and asked for their help in dealing with the bills and so many people would have given their help.

Jim had asked me back in October when I was still very ill if we needed any financial help but I had seen my wife the night before and she told me that everything was under control, so I told him at that time to touch base with her to if she needed any help. I knew that over the last few months friends from our two church's had been extremely generous and had been giving to my wife almost every week while I was ill, so to be so far behind with all the bills just did not add up. As the news of how much debt we were in hit me I felt as though the storm clouds were just growing ever thicker, yet God had another plan, at exactly the time that my Stepfather and Jim had been made aware of all the debt the Lord provided

PSALM 68 VERSE 10 thou O God, hast prepared of thy goodness for the poor

Just about all of our debts would be covered by Gods gracious hand as some money had amazingly been given to us as a family. Once again I found myself feeling overwhelmed by Gods merciful hand at work in my life, he truly knows all of our problems, all we have to do is put our faith in him, to trust him whole heartedly. I gave my stepfather full control of our finances so that he could pay off the debts. It had been a very difficult afternoon finding out how much financial trouble we were in and my wife was visiting me that evening along with our children. A thousand thoughts raced through my mind, some of them not so nice as anger tried to take control of me over the mess we were in. I wondered about how tough I should be with her. Our marriage was already hanging together by the thinnest of strands as it was, without these financial problems to deal with as well! After they had gone that afternoon I sat quietly in prayer over what to say to my wife, I asked God to give me the right words to say when I saw her later on that night. In Matthew 7 verse 7 the bible says, Ask and it will be given to you; seek and you will find.

That evening when my wife arrived to see me, she was unusually calm she had very little to say, it was as though God had closed her mouth and had told her to listen. I began by asking if she knew how much debt we were in, she just shook her head as if in denial. When I spelled it out to her she reacted like it was a complete shock to her. Her reaction was no surprise to me as my stepfather had told me that he had found a drawer of unopened mail at our house when he had gone round to see her one day.

I then asked her why she had allowed things like the water bill to fall so far behind again after I had worked so hard to straighten it out. my wife immediately went very defensive, defending her actions telling me how much she had been struggling to pay the bills as it was. She went on to remind me that she was having to feed our two children on what benefits she was on while I was ill. I explained to her that I knew that friends of ours were helping so much and told her that all she had to do was ask for Jim or my stepfather David to help and they would readily have jumped in to support her in any way they could. My wife was having none of that though and told me that she did not like Jim or my stepfather interfering as it was our business not theirs. I tried to ask her about other debts that had mounted up, but she just defended herself and then blamed the company's we owed money to for sending letters demanding payment. I could not believe what I hearing, I tried to change tack and told her that some of the debt was mine as there were bills going out of my account that she no control over, and since I had been in hospital now nearly three months I was no longer receiving sick pay so bills in my account were no longer being covered. My wife though had now put up a smoke screen and was denying any wrong doing on her part for the mess we were in.

I realised I was on a hiding to nothing trying to reason with her over it, there was no moving her so I told her that I had put David in charge of sorting out the mess we were in and told her that in all probability we would be almost debt free once he had gone through all of our finances and paid the bills for us. I explained that we had to straighten out our financial situation before I was well enough to come home because once I was home things were going to be tough enough with me not being able to work for some considerable time anyway. The mention of David intervening annoyed her, she angrily said to me, why are you letting David interfere with our marriage its got nothing to do with him. It was true it did have nothing to do with him but he cared about us so much and everything I had seen so far told me that my wife needed help especially with the finances.

She stormed off that evening without even a goodbye or a kiss, I felt as though I was constantly being battered by storms of my wife's making. Whatever I did do was wrong in her eyes. She made it plain as daylight that it was my fault that Jim and my family had met to discuss our finances and had not invited her to the meeting, it left me feeling totally helpless being stuck in hospital.

All the stress of what was going on was affecting me on a physical front, their were days where I found myself at times unable or unwilling to push myself hard to make physical leaps forward, in truth I was feeling totally demoralised with it all. My body was not responding quickly to treatment or therapy and even on days where I did put all my effort into trying to get better, my body would so often refuse to cooperate with what I was doing in therapy sessions. Every day during the week I had physio sessions and much of what we worked on was my core stability and arm exercises, my legs were still at a point where their was no movement in them at all. One of the physio assistants (Sarah) who I worked with daily would go through all of my exercises with me, which were quite extensive and they did go as far as moving my legs up and down. My upper body was doing really well and with assistance from Sarah, my arm exercises were getting easier week by week, but my legs were still not doing anything and Sarah was doing all the work lifting my legs, I could see that my legs must have weighed a lot as Sarah always seemed very happy when we had gotten my leg exercises out of the way. I still could not lift my arms above my head and the slow progress often left me feeling really unhappy, I found that the only thing I could do was turn to Jesus and lay all of my burdens upon him and right at this time I had so many burdens. I truly did not know which way to turn where my marriage was concerned and the revelation of all the financial mess we were in had only made things worse as my wife accepted no responsibility over them. I knew how much all of the strain was affecting me so I laid it all at the foot of the cross and asked God to help me. PSALM 146 VERSE 5, Happy is he that hath the God of Jacob for his help, whose hope is in the Lord his God.

Although I was feeling completely frustrated with everything, God was giving me the inner strength to get through each day, and although my physical progress was painfully slow progress was progress. There was now only about a week to go to Christmas, my left arm had progressed so well over that month I had been at the Devonshire unit that with the help of some foam aids I was now able to feed myself. Up until then I had had to rely upon the staff feeding me at dinner times but now providing my food was cut up for me I was able to do it myself. I still struggled with things like mashed potato as the consistency was often too thick for me to be able to push a fork into but it was a great feeling to be able to fend for myself a little. Guillain-Barre syndrome really does strip everything away, I found myself amazed at how special and wonderful the human body is, what a wonder of creation we are, that God made us and gave us such abilities. Every little movement we make is amazing. Having an illness like Guillain-Barre where you end up in a state of paralysis makes you appreciate even the slightest movement that your body makes. Many times I would be sat trying to perform a simple task like turning pages of a book or magazine and I would fail as my arms and hands were not strong enough and I would after just a few minutes of trying end up feeling completely exhausted.

Whenever I finally managed to perform a task that I may have been working on for some time, I always felt that God should take the praise for it, and often on quiet afternoons I would be drawn to sing songs in praise of what God was doing in my life. I also now found myself singing songs that were coming straight from my own heart, God was laying so much song in my heart and I yearned to be able to play my guitar again. I had a small note pad and I now began using it to write down some of the songs that I was singing out to God, being able to play guitar was still some way off but nothing was going to stop me singing out to glorify Gods holy name.

Again I found that God was drawing so close to me through all the troubles I had, but not only was he comforting me and caring for me he was now giving me a gift of song and I found that being able to praise God despite all the heartache and pain was one of the best medicines I had every day.

CHAPTER 5

CHRISTMAS 2008

Christmas was racing up upon me, and my room mate Barry had been given a week at home to see how he and his wife would cope so I was back to living on my own for a little while. I had gotten used to having somebody to talk to each day so now being on my own I felt lonely again, I was always so blessed though as friends and family continued to visit me taking time out of their busy lives to come all the way to see me.

My mum was visiting me three times a week and during the week on the run up to Christmas she told me that she and my stepfather had arranged with the staff in the hospital that I could go out to their house for Christmas day, It was the best news I had had in weeks, it felt so special to be able to spend Christmas day with my family and knowing also that my wife and children would be their too just left me feeling so blessed. This was going to be the first time I had spent a day away from the hospital since being admitted and I was really excited about it.

When my wife visited me a day later I told her the news of what was happening on Christmas day and she seemed genuinely pleased that we would be able to spend Christmas day together as a family. Having all the debt hanging around our necks did leave us financially in all sorts of trouble and it looked as though the children would have to make do with very small presents that year as we just did not have the money. I knew the money situation was really affecting my wife and she seemed really depressed about it and it was hurting me too knowing that we could not afford to buy presents for the children. Unknown to me at that point the Anglican church on the estate where we lived had given my wife fifty pounds worth of shopping vouchers so that she could buy toys for our two children for Christmas, the level of love being poured out for us as a family was just staggering. Even today when I look back on what everybody was doing for us as a family it still moves me to the point of tears, but I also look back upon it and can see that it was God who was stirring everybody's hearts to continue pouring their love out in his name. God really does care for us through all of our troubles and wants to bless us and for us to know his love and experience it and I was getting a fresh outpouring of his love daily.

On the run up to Christmas day members of staff from the hospital and a church that was close by had all come into the hospital to sing Christmas carols to the patients. Christmas is such a special time of the year for me and hearing all the carols that I had sung in church as young boy when I was in the choir at St Luke's was a lovely thing for me that Christmas. During all my years in the armed forces and a few years beyond that I had turned my back upon God and Christmas had during those years become an excuse to go out and get drunk and have a party. The true meaning of Christmas in truth had been lost on me until I turned back to God in 2006. But now having spent two years back in church and getting to know God again I began to understand what it was truly about. Christmas still is a time to celebrate for me but not for myself but for Jesus who came to earth as a babe, the light of the world who took upon himself all of my sins as well as yours so that we can have a relationship with the father through him and be washed clean of all our sins.

Celebrating the birth of the messiah is now more important to me than receiving gifts and yet that is exactly what God gave to us a gift, JESUS! I so often feel really humbled that God has given us the greatest gift of all, all we have to do is turn to Jesus in faith, in truth and in love and ask that he take away our sins and for us to truly repent of all we have done and it will be done it is amazing grace.

On Christmas day two nurses came to get me ready for my day out at my mums house, a taxi had been booked to come and pick me up around eleven in the morning. All of the staff were in high spirits that morning and wished all the patients a very happy Christmas. It always saddened me to think that people had to work on Christmas day but without the staff's loving care and hard work on these days the patients simply would not get fed or dressed or be given medication and I always look upon the work that they did as very sacrificial in the way they gave up family time for the job that they did. I was soon hoisted into my wheelchair so that I was ready for when my taxi would arrive to take me to my mums house. I sat there that morning reading my bible and every few minutes I kept looking up at the clock to see what time it was. The time seemed to be going so slowly and the excitement I felt in the pit of my stomach was growing ever more as the clock ticked closer and closer to eleven. The room I had at the hospital was opposite the entrance to the building so I could often see the cars coming and going from the hospital and almost on the dot at eleven that morning I saw a taxi cab arrive. Seeing a taxi cab surprised me as I had been expecting all morning a small van that had its own integral ramp fitted at the rear designed purposely for wheelchairs. I began wondering how I was going to get into the taxi. A member of the nursing staff came and put my coat on and gave me all the medication that I needed to take with me for the day and then wheeled me around to the buildings entrance, as I wheeled through all of the staff and other patients I met along the way wished me a happy Christmas and told me to enjoy my day out with my family.

As we arrived at the door my curiosity of how I was going to get in to the taxi was satisfied as the driver had attached two little ramps to get me in, the taxi driver took over from the nurse and with one heave he pushed me into the vehicle and then clamped my wheelchair in. I chatted with the taxi driver all the way to my mums house whilst all the while looking out of the windows taking in the beautiful scenery we were driving through, a few months ago before falling ill I would have thought nothing about taking a walk in the hills that surrounded the area we lived in. Yet here I found myself just marvelling at the open countryside that I could see. Having spent nearly a whole three months in hospital only seeing the outdoors when I looked out of a window or when I had been transferred across from one hospital to the next really made me appreciate what I was seeing and left me appreciating just what a wonderful creation the world is and how beautiful God had made it. I had always loved the great outdoors and it was one of the reasons that I had joined the army back in the nineties, so I could see a bit of the world whilst I worked and I had been greatly blessed by God with that. I had lived in Germany for nearly five years and whilst there I had travelled to Canada a number of times for various training purposes, and also been to a lot of European countries too. But travelling out the four or five miles to my mums house that Christmas morning it felt as though I was rediscovering the world. I had spent so long cooped up in hospital that I had almost forgotten what it was like on the outside and every turn on the roads to my mums house brought a new revelation in to my sight, it was such a wonderful thing to savour and I felt in awe of God for the beauty around me.

The journey in all took about half an hour as the roads were so quiet, the taxi driver was not all that certain about where my mums house was. He had the address but had only occasionally ventured this far out from the Stockport area so I assisted him in finding my mums house. My stepfather David came out to meet me as the taxi driver wheeled me out of his vehicle and he told the driver he would ring him later on that afternoon when I was ready to go back to hospital. David wheeled me around to the back of the house and he had made a makeshift ramp to get me into their dinning room through the patio doors. It took a couple of efforts to get me into the dinning room but eventually I was in. My wife and children were already there to meet me and my son came running into the room to give me a big hug followed by my wife and my now eight month old daughter all wishing me a happy Christmas. It really felt so special to be spending Christmas day with them.

Just then my wife gave me a real surprise as she had a present for me I truly had not expected one as I knew how tight our finances were and I had myself only just managed with the help of my mum to buy my wife some perfume for Christmas. My hands were still not strong enough to open the wrapping on the present so my wife had to do it for me, I was completely astounded when she opened the box to see a watch that looked very expensive. It was a beautiful watch and I thanked her for it and gave her a hug she told me that she and the children wanted to get me something really special for Christmas as I had been through so much these last few months, my wife left me alone for a few moments and I was almost in tears as I sat there alone. I was completely shocked, I could not understand how she had managed to afford this watch with our finances already so stretched.

A short while later my elder brother and his wife Claire and their two children arrived and it was great to see Claire and the girls as I had not seen them since falling ill, my elder brother Paul was coming to see me regularly as he always came on Wednesday afternoons on his way home from work. My mum had put together a really lovely Christmas dinner with all the trimmings and we all sat around the table in the dinning room enjoying our festive meal, It felt so good to be there with them, only a week before I had had no idea that it was even possible for me to be able to spend the day with them. Eating a meal was still an exercise all of its own and I had to rely upon my mum to cut my food up for me so that I could then feed myself but it was a joy to be able to do even that.

After we had all enjoyed dinner together there was the small matter of getting through to my mums living room, the door way that led from the dinning room was too small to get my wheelchair through, so David and my brother Paul worked together to get me back out of the patio door. They wheeled me around to the front of the property to the front door. But still there was obstacles to negotiate as my mums house has three steps at the front, between them they heaved me up the stone steps and into the living room. It was all quite an operation and I felt rather guilty just sat there as they did all the work, it was exactly the kind of thing I would have gotten stuck right in to doing so having to sit back and be the watcher/ patient was always a difficult thing for me to grasp. We had a lovely afternoon together as we watched the Queens speech and then a movie together, it was wonderful watching my son playing with his new toys and I loved all the cuddles I got with my daughter. My wife seemed to enjoy the time we had on Christmas day together although I know that she would have preferred it if we could have had more time together than just the day, I was still not well enough to spend long periods of time out of hospital and the rehabilitation of my body was in all honesty still in its infancy, I still had a long road to go down before I could seriously be looking at a possible discharge date from hospital but spending Christmas day with my family really gave me the spur to work doubly hard at getting better.

The afternoon went so quickly and by about four in the afternoon I was feeling worn out, I was becoming very uncomfortable. I knew it was time to ask David if he could ring for the taxi to come and pick me up, I had about a half hour wait before the taxi would arrive and I savoured that extra time I did get with my wife and children on Christmas day before I had to go. All in all it had been a lovely day although very tiring for me and as David and my brother Paul got me down the steps again I could feel my body aching ever more with every bounce down the steps. My son came and gave me a big hug and kiss, but my wife seemed reluctant to come and say goodbye to me, it was only through my mums prompting that she actually came over and gave me a peck on the cheek. Her love for me at that moment felt so icy cold it was as though she wanted nothing more to do with me.

As I travelled back to hospital in the taxi I felt so sad and lost, I should have felt happy that I had just spent the day with my family, but instead my feelings of anguish over my marriage just spilled forth. I often felt so helpless being in hospital and not being able to do anything about the state of my marriage. I often prayed to God for clear guidance over what to do and how to approach trying to rekindle the sense of love we had once had for each other. Yet I felt as though I was banging my head against a brick wall with her, nothing I said seemed to make any difference and it all left me feeling as though I was wasting my time.

I was so glad when I arrived back at the hospital, Bob was on hand straight away and he quickly got me hoisted back into bed as he could see how uncomfortable I was. As he lowered me into my bed and the mattress took my weight the feeling of relief was wonderful. For the last hour my body had been screaming at me I was so grateful to be back in bed it had been the busiest day I had had since falling ill, and I felt really tired. Bob lifted the headrest on my bed so I could lie there semi sat up and he then put my bed table across the bed for me so I could read. My mum had sent me back to the hospital with a couple of sandwiches to eat and I was now hungry enough to eat them so I asked Bob before he left my room if he would open the foil for me so that I could tuck into them, I had physically come so far over the last month and to think that when I arrived at the Devonshire unit I could only just move my left arm! But now I was able to feed myself and write with my left hand, but opening things was still a little too complicated for me to manage.

My thoughts that evening were preoccupied with how my wife had seemed reluctant to even come and give me a kiss or a hug before I went back to hospital and in truth she had been very quiet all day and had not said much to me. The more I looked for a solution the less I found one, I felt guilty that I had not bought my wife an expensive present yet I knew that the reason was that I could not afford to do so. Over the years that we had been together I had always bought her a new phone or a piece of jewellery for Christmas so to not have those gifts I assumed can only have hurt her. I knew though that we truly were in a place where we could end up sinking financially and I placed greater emphasis on our future financial stability, I wanted us to have a future where debt was not hanging around our necks.

MATTHEW 6 VERSES 19 & 20, lay not up for yourselves treasures upon earth, where moth and rust doth corrupt and where thieves break through and steal, but lay up for yourselves treasures in heaven where neither moth nor rust doth corrupt and where thieves do not break through nor steal.

CHAPTER 6

VISION OF TROUBLE AHEAD

The new year began really positively, feeding myself was getting much easier and my right arm despite still being significantly weaker than my left in strength was now starting to become useful again and I was able to hold very light things in it like a knife to aid with cutting food. I was still at a place where cutting food up was really hard for me to do but it was all about getting my arms used to doing things again and every time I tried a particular task like trying to cut food up I found that I got better at it. I was also writing very well with my left hand and Ruth had bought me a little gift of a diary for the new year and each day I was now writing down my thoughts and physical progress in it, the diary was such a valuable tool not only in writing this book but in getting my hand writing really good again. I always joke now that God wanted to do something so radical with me that one of the improvements to my life that he has given me was to sort out my awful spidery scrawly handwriting that I used to have.

During the second week of January 2009 I had a team meeting with the doctors, nursing staff and therapy staff, the aim of the meeting is to basically go over how therapy has gone and to get some clear goals from the patient for the staff so they can tailor your therapy to work on the things that are important to you. My mum and stepfather arrived for the meeting followed shortly afterwards by my wife, one of the things that the hospital like to do is involve your family in this process as it helps them understand how therapy is going and where it is going. So often it can be a great encouragement for them to hear how the staff feel the therapy is working for their family member who is ill.

Me and my family sat chatting while the doctors and therapy staff began the meeting, it gave the staff time to look through my medical notes and to make a plan of therapy to undertake over the next few months. Finally the nurse who was in the meeting came to get us, my mum pushed me down the corridor and my wife wheeled my daughter down in her buggy. Each of the different heads of departments who were in the meeting talked about how my care and therapy was going and in most cases I was making good progress, the nurses were happy as I was medically stable. I still needed their help with things like washing and dressing and bathing but in general terms I was heading in the right direction.

The occupational therapist said that all the work with them so far had been slow but that they were pleased that I had come on and was now able to feed myself with a little help and that my ability to write left handed was very impressive, something that she told me not many people can do after being right handed all their lives. Next was the turn of Mark my physio, he explained that although physical progress was painfully slow he was pleased as I was making progress and my arms were improving all the time, he also said that my core muscles were beginning to get stronger as I was now able to do mini crunches sat in my wheelchair. So all in all although painfully slow I was physically improving. Before the meeting had taken place the staff had given me a little questionnaire to fill out. this was so that I could tell them my goals and priorities for my recovery. Mark my physio had hold of that questionnaire, he looked through my goals and read them out one by one. My number one aim was to be able to walk again and Mark sat there and told us all that he felt that it was a very realistic aim, it did mean that a lot of hard work was going to have be done to achieve that aim both by me and the physio staff but he felt that it was still very achievable.

My number two aim was to gain more independence in all areas, this again would mean working hard on things like being able to care for myself, washing and dressing, having a shave etc. Mark felt that if I continue to show the same level of improvement in being able to do things for myself then that would not be a problem either. My long term goal was to be able to spend more time with my family. The last few months had been very difficult for me, Being cut off from my family and I longed to be well enough to spend at least a weekend away from hospital with them.

Faith—Through the storm

This aim my doctor talked to me about and she felt that at the moment I was still quite a way off being able to spend time away from the hospital but that in a few months time it might be a realistic option.

The final aim that I had was to be able to play my guitar again, this for me had been very frustrating having hands that do not do what you want them to do. None of the staff had ever played an instrument so this was going to be down to me and I said as much in the meeting myself. The staff were more than happy for me to have my guitar in the hospital in my room so that I could start working with it so I asked my wife to bring my guitar in for me the next time she visited.

The meeting had been a real eye opener for me as to how well I was doing in recovery from Guillain-barre and at times it felt really strange to hear people talking about me and how my treatment was going, but the overall feeling I got from the meeting was that the staff were pleased with the progress that I was making and that with hard work all of my goals were possible. It was lovely having family with me for the meeting and it really meant a lot to me.

My wife was really against David helping us and truly did not like anyone else being involved, and it always hurt me that she felt that way. She struggled with accepting help from people though I felt it was what she needed and I often bore the brunt of her anger with that. She often said to me angrily, why are you letting these people interfere with our marriage, your married to me not them. All I could see was how much everybody was doing to help us and that their love being poured out into our marriage not to interfere but to give us the help and support that we needed during this difficult time. One of the things that I always found strange was the fact that if she was left to get on with it at home she would come to see me moaning that no one had been down to help her. One evening when Ruth came to see me I explained what my wife had told me about people not helping her, Ruth told me that that was just not true! she was constantly receiving help from our friends, I truly felt that I was between a rock and a hard place with my wife. No matter which way I turned it seemed that I could not please her or give her what she was after, I found it all very confusing that she was in effect behaving so badly and always bringing more hurt into an already difficult time.

Having visitors always helped getting me away from the frustration of being in hospital and a new visitor started to come to see me on Monday evenings, Mark was a friend from our sister church. Those Monday evenings were always good fun with Mark he was never the sort of guy to just sit there and chat for a while and on his first visit to see me he had gone and found the hospitals chess set so that we could have a game while we sat and chatted. I had not played chess since I was a boy so I have to say that I was very rusty to begin wit. When Mark had stated visiting me I was still too weak to pick up the pieces myself and move them on the board so Mark had had to do it for me, but by the middle of January I was able with my left arm to just about move them myself. Mark commented on what a great improvement I had made in just the short time he had been coming to see me and said how impressed he was by it. I have to say that Mark was probably far less impressed with my chess skills in all the weeks that he had been coming to see me, he had won every time, but as the weeks went by I gradually got better and was by the end of January starting to give him a better match when we played.

The Lord was so close to me and I had a real conviction in my heart that he wanted me to be working directly for him in some capacity or other, I somehow knew that I would never drive a lorry again to earn a living but that God had plans for my life that were very different from what I was used to. Music had always been a real love of mine and the evening that my wife brought my guitar in I could not wait to see if I could play any notes on it. Billy one of my closest friends from church had brought my wife up to see that evening and he brought my guitar across to me while I sat resting back on my bed, he put it across my lap in the usual playing position and I had my first go at playing it. At first I tried down the bottom of the neck but could not even get a note out of it, my fingers were just not strong enough. So I moved my left hand up the neck to about the twelfth fret and pressed down as hard as I could on the lowest string of the neck and picked the string with my right hand, I just about got a note out of it before my left hand gave up due to muscle fatigue. It was terribly frustrating and my wife said that she did not see the point of me having it at hospital if I could not play it. I felt that that was wrong I needed a positive attitude towards trying to play again and I needed to pick it back up and keep trying, I was so determined that I would play guitar again.

The Lord was also laying so many songs in my heart that at different times of the day I would find myself singing and many a melody I would record onto my phone so I could remember it or I would scribble it down into my notepad, I felt so at peace with God his love was just pouring out, washing me afresh from all the pain and suffering I was enduring I have very few words that can describe how I was feeling other than I just felt so loved by God and felt so on fire for him.

PSALM 149, Praise ye the Lord, sing unto the Lord a new song.

In my therapy sessions Mark was now very keen to work on getting me stood up and introduced me to a wooden frame. I was hoisted onto a plinth in the gym and I sat on the end of it. The frame was then pushed in front of me, in all I had three physio;s working with me in these sessions. Two behind me pushing me up from my waist and one in front working on getting my knee's to straighten. I sat there a few moments composing myself like a top athlete which I certainly was not. I counted down from three and then gave it my all to get stood up, on the first attempt the physio;s let me see if I could do it but my body was so weak that I ended up just sitting there not going anywhere, yet I felt as though I had just exerted the most effort ever in my life. I had a short rest again gathering my energy for another attempt, Mark told the girls working behind me to give me as much help as needed to get me stood up. I counted down again and gave as much as I could Mark and his assistants put in all the work and got me stood up, the feeling of being stood up though on my own two feet was one of pure pleasure it felt wonderful, months of being sat down and small, I now felt like a giant. Without the physio;s propping me up it would never have happened but the feeling was just amazing and I was left feeling elated about it for the rest of the day.

Mark explained that although he and his assistants were doing ninety five percent of the work to get me stood up he said that it was imperative that we continued doing it in future physio sessions as it would most probably wake up sleeping muscles that had gotten used to being immobile over the last few months. I knew that without the work the physio;s were doing I would have just fallen to the floor in a crumpled heap and caused myself more injury but Despite the fact that the physio;s were doing ninety five percent of the work in these sessions I always felt really drained afterwards. My body's response to any physical work was to leave me feeling exhausted. I often needed to rest after a session in the gym just so that I had the strength to get through the rest of the day, it seemed so strange to be so exhausted I had always been really fit. I was left in awe of just how wonderful our bodies are. Having such a debilitating illness really left me marvelling at what an amazing creation we are, that may sound strange as my body was so weak but every little movement that

I got back really amazed me and blessed me so much and it gave me an understanding of what an amazing thing God did in making us.

On January the seventeenth the most amazing thing happened to me, it was a Saturday and at weekends there was no therapy sessions so they tended to be quiet, I remember waking that morning and starting my day with prayer, I prayed over all the problems that I had and was still facing. I particularly prayed for my family and that mornings prayer time left me feeling so at peace, God has a way of bringing peace even when we seem to be in the middle of a storm and I truly felt thankful for the daily doses I was receiving I felt like I needed them more than ever. The weekends were always slow and my wife was now visiting me on a Friday evening with the children so it was quite usual for me to spend Saturday on my own and sometimes even Sundays, I found those times alone to be a great way to spend time with God as the usual hustle and bustle on the wards was even quieter and I could even close off what noise there was on the ward by having my room door closed.

I had since Ruth had brought me a bible in to read really gotten stuck into reading it and was already reading the book of Job having started in Genesis. I had never just picked up my bible before and just read it from the front cover, but it seemed the perfect thing to do now and I was truly enjoying it. The book of Job had become such a wonderful one for me as right from the start of my illness I had quoted Job as to how I felt about what was happening with my illness.

The enemy said in Job that he could get Job to curse God and God had taken Satan up on his wager, I was not certain that that was what was happening with me, but I knew one thing for sure, I had come under attack because the enemy did not want me to have a loving relationship with Jesus. He wanted me to curse God and to blame God for my illness, he wanted me to fall far away from God. I felt that this was truly his plot, the enemy does not see the end result though he only sees what harm he can do provided you let the things that happen to you affect you. His attacks upon my health and then upon my marriage only strengthened my love of God. In all honesty all the attacks I had come under up to that point were all designed or manipulated to drive me away from God, but his tactic actually had the exact opposite affect upon me. He had driven me too Jesus not away from him. Having attacked me first Satan then turned his attention upon my wife to try to get to me, my wife being a fairly young Christian had given in to what temptations had been laid before her. Often when she came to see me she would say to me that she did not understand how I could believe that God existed after what had happened to me. Her faith in God seemed to have ebbed away and try as I might to show her that Jesus was the reason I was still alive and slowly recovering, she seemed to have closed her ears to what I had to say.

I sat that Saturday evening and watched football highlights on TV before calling it a night to get some sleep, my daily routine now was to spend most of the day in my wheelchair and then after tea be hoisted back into bed. The nursing staff were by now very used to my routine and each night when I was ready to go to sleep they would come in and put the back rest down on my bed so I could lie flat. Sleeping was still a problem occasionally as nerve pain could and would disrupt my sleep, but on the whole I was sleeping much better than I had when I was in Hope hospital.

My hospital room that night was in complete darkness but for the light shining in through the portal shaped window in the door. I was fast asleep but around three a.m a strange noise that I could not pinpoint woke me from my sleep, I lay there for a few moments with my eyes wide open, trying to work out what the noise was. The sound I was hearing intensified and then suddenly just above my head a bright white light shone out in the darkness of my room. I had not turned on any lights and neither had a nurse been in to do so. I lay there feeling fearful of what I was seeing and experiencing, in all my life nothing quite like this had ever happened and for a few moments I did not know what to make of it.

Almost as quickly as it had appeared it was gone, and I was left lying there for a few moments wondering what had just happened. I wondered for a moment if the bed side light had somehow managed to turn itself on, but the light had not emanated from the lamp. It had appeared to hover above my head before just suddenly disappearing again, I stayed awake for the next hour or so praying to God asking for his insight in to what had just happened as I could make no sense of it myself. Listening for Gods voice was something that before my illness had at times seemed alien to me but over the course of the next few days I heard from God more clearly than ever. He told me that what had happened that night was a gift from him to me, God did not go on to tell me what the gift was but he told me that I must trust him as all would be revealed.

I had a real sense of Gods love for me, more than ever I felt Gods presence and had days where I could sit in my wheelchair and feel such joy in my heart over what had taken place that night, it had at the time frightened me beyond anything I had experienced before, but God telling me that it was a gift was enough for me to know that I had been blessed.

ACTS 1 verse 8, But ye shall receive power after that the Holy ghost is come upon you.

I was completely astounded by what had happened that night, I had heard of people having encounters like this with God but was never truly sure about them happening and now I was the one that it had happened to. I could no longer push these things aside as a myth, we all too often try to deny something like this could happen and then God comes along and blows our earthly understanding completely out of the water and teaches us something new about himself.

MATTHEW 14 VERSE 31, O though of little faith, wherefore didst thou doubt?

Physio sessions were now more than ever geared towards getting me up and on my feet and every day I was having a session with them to continue working on standing up. On top of those daily sessions I was also having a daily dose of going through my exercises with Sarah, usually after lunch. These sessions took in all aspects of my recovery from my legs to my arms to work on my core muscles, Sarah was always a hard task master and expected you to put a hundred percent in to your exercises every time. It was good to have someone who was not afraid of pushing you to the limit of what you could do and she always had a smile on her face when she was telling me to work harder.

Mark often gave Sarah new exercises to get me to do and one of those new exercises was to try and get myself up from my bed using my arms. This particular exercise involved me being side ways on to my bed sat in my wheelchair with the arm of the wheelchair removed so that I could lean over to the bed and rest my head and torso on the bed. I was then to attempt to get myself sat back upright in the wheelchair from this position using my arms and trunk muscles. At first when we began this exercise I could not do it without help from Sarah and we found that when we turned around to do it with my right hip closest to the floor searing pain would tear through that hip leaving me in too much pain to continue with my physio. I would always manage once on that side when we did the exercise but more than that was just too much for me to bear.

As the weeks passed by this exercise slowly got easier to do and I was by the end of January I was getting part way up on my own before Sarah's help was needed, on the downside of things my right hip was giving me so much pain that it often prevented me from even starting the exercise which often left me feeling really disappointed and frustrated that it was stopping my therapy sessions. I decided that I needed to talk to my doctor when she did her walk round on the ward and after talking with her about it she told me that she felt there was a drug she could give me that would help with the pain. I was sure that if someone picked me up I would rattle with the amount of medication I was on. Wonderfully this new drug had within a few days taken the edge off the pain in my hip and I was now able to do the exercise without feeling the pain right away and could at least attempt a few times before it got too much, although the pain was still there it was much dissipated from what it had been I was so glad to be able to continue my therapy sessions instead of having to cut them short.

My arms were getting much stronger and the range of movement in them was getting slightly better week by week, my only problem was that my hands lagged far behind in the range of movement they had. Yes I was now able to write (left handed) and able to turn pages in books with some difficulty but lifting things was a huge problem. I had a pile of books that I kept on my table and I would often end up knocking one of them on the floor as I tried to get one to read, which would end up with me pressing my call bell so a nurse would come to pick it up for me. The very process of pressing my call bell was interesting in itself as basically the call bell was laid on my bed next to me and from there it was a case of lifting my arm as high as I could and then just dropping my arm onto the switch. I often needed a couple of attempts to manage to do it but there was no other way as my fingers were not strong enough to even press the switch. The thing that did work work for me was to let gravity do the work as my arm came crashing down on the switch. It was often the case that the one book I wanted to read would be the one book that I had knocked on the floor. The nurses were always great about it and even joked with me that I did it on purpose just so they had to come and tend to me, one of the health care assistants in particular would put her head around the door and look at me with her best serious expression and say "buzzers are not toys" She always made me laugh with her witty remarks, and after she had helped me out with what ever I had needed doing she would cancel my call bell and tell me not to ring it again, jokingly! Although I am sure she would say even now that she was not joking as that was all part of the joke.

Jez Smith

    The physical difficulties that I still had almost four months on from having first fallen ill and been paralysed from the neck down were frustrating to me at times, it sometimes felt as though all the hard work that I was putting in was completely fruitless. It often took weeks to even see the slightest improvement physically, I cant begin to tell you how discouraging that was. Despite how frustrating it was the only thing I could was put all my faith in God that he would heal me. I often think about how for some people a recovery from paralysis is not even an option and yet here I was by the grace of God given that very opportunity. Many of my friends who came to visit me in hospital would say what an encouragement I was to them, they often told me of how members of our church were being greatly strengthened by how God was at work in my life and that it gave them courage too. I never knew what to say to them when they said these things, it was always a huge surprise for me to hear that people were being strengthened in this way, just by what I was going through. In 2 Corinthians 12 verse 10 it says, therefore I take pleasure in infirmities, in reproaches, in necessities, in persecutions, in distresses for Christ's sake for when I am weak then I am strong. Also in Romans 15 verse 14 it says, for everything that was written in the past was written to teach us, so that through endurance and the encouragement of the scriptures we might have hope. Despite how weak I was, despite all the pain God was using me even from my hospital bed as an example and giving strength to others. I felt so blown away by what God was doing, he brings good out of even the most desperate of situations and it brought me to a place where I felt so in awe of his power and his grace at work in my life.

    On Tuesday January the twentieth I woke from sleep around six thirty in the morning and started my day as usual with a time of prayer after that I just lay there before the Lord quietly, I felt the Lords peace rush over me and it was a moment of great wonder that morning. As I lay there still, my mind seemed to be overwhelmed with images, a vision from God! I could see Jesus on the cross he was in pain but in glory at the same time, I found myself facing Jesus and then realised that I too was on a cross with my arms stretched out. I looked to my left to find my wife also on a cross facing Jesus and then to the ground and I could see thousands and thousands of people stood staring up at us they were shouting and singing praises to the Lord and encouraging us to come and follow Jesus. I lifted my gaze back up and stared at Jesus and he looked into my eyes and he said to me "come follow me for I am the way, the truth and the light".

Without any hesitation I found myself suddenly free of the cross and I was walking through the air towards Jesus giving my life to him, when suddenly from behind me to my left all I could hear was wailing and screaming. My wife was crying and she screamed out "I can't do this" at that moment the vision ended. I opened my eyes and lay there wondering what this vision had meant, did it forecast more marital problems or that I must do more to bring my wife back to the Lords loving comfort. I just did not know, in many ways the vision had frightened me and I went into a time of prayer asking God for forgiveness for me and my wife, and I asked God to reveal to me what this vision meant.

The rest of that week continued with lots of physio sessions and lots of visitors, my mum and stepfather visited as did my pastor Jim and Paul and Andrew from church on the Wednesday afternoon, my elder brother Paul also arrived shortly after everyone else. I was having a physio session that afternoon when they arrived and I was in the gym, Mark asked me if I was OK with them all being in the room at the same time and I was fine with it. He then explained to them what I was about to do. I was hooked up to a machine that aids in sitting to standing called the Encore. I was sat down in my wheelchair with a harness around me that was attached to the machine, the Encore was positioned in front of me and had two arms that extended out towards me with handles on it.

After Mark had told everyone what the machine did and how it would hopefully help me to regain strength we set about doing this new exercise. Sarah was also working with Mark that afternoon. She was behind me to help me get up as I was still a long way off being able to do this exercise without assistance. The problem I was having was being able to hold onto the handles without losing my grip as it went upwards so some assistance was needed with this. Mark asked me if I was ready to go and I was as ready as ever, Sarah gave me as much help as needed and before I knew it I was stood up with only the minimal amount of assistance from Sarah to keep me steady. The feeling of being stood up was just amazing and I looked around at my family and friends and I could see that they too felt amazed at what they were seeing. I soon needed to sit back down as fatigue quickly took over.

However I was not finished yet, I sat there mustering all my strength for another go whilst chatting with everyone. I remember Andrew saying that it was amazing to see me do that and I felt good to be sharing my healing with them, showing them the awesome healing Jesus was bringing to my body. I stood another two times during that session and truly felt so amazed to have managed so much that day. My friends told me that I was a great encouragement to them that afternoon. Often my friends could see so much better than me just how far I had come and how well I was doing since the last time they had visited me, afterwards we all went back to my room and chatted for a while before visiting time was over. It was a really wonderful day and I gained so much strength from what I had achieved that day. I felt that I had made a really big break through with my physio and was deeply encouraged by my friends and family as they all seemed so positive about what they had seen me do that afternoon, but if anyone deserved the credit for what I was now achieving in physio it was Jesus, he was the one that had saved me and he was the one now giving me healing and he was giving me the strength to get through the storm.

Every week when my brother visited me invariably he had a letter with him from his wife which he would read out while he was with me and then give to me to look over and then read at my own leisure, often the letters had some story of humour in them about what my brother had gotten up to or their two children but this one was different this one was had a message within it that completely amazed me.

Claire's own words from a letter dated the 6/1/09.

This week I think its time to let you know about when you were in intensive care at Hope hospital. You were so poorly and we were all obviously very worried and concerned if you would pull through. After saying a few prayers I opened my good news bible at where the ribbon book mark was—hoping to read something of comfort or reassurance. Job 17 verse 1, was where it opened but I ended up in tears as I read what it said: "The end of my life is near. I can hardly breath; there is nothing left for me but the grave."

I was of course rather upset to read this . . . especially as your breathing was causing a big problem at that time. So I asked in another prayer, if there was something else for me to read, that I would be shown it when I opened my bible again, (I must admit though that I was a bit worried about what I would read). The next page I opened my little good news bible at was Matthew 9. I did not need to read past the subheading JESUS HEALS A PARALYSED MAN.

I felt so amazed at what my brother had just read out, my sister in law had made those prayers on the night that I was taken up to intensive care. I knew that God had listened to all the prayers that had been offered up for me when I was so ill, but just getting this first hand account of how God had answered my own sister in laws prayers completely astonished me. It was as though God was showing her the very battle that I was facing, that I was so short of breath. Then in her next prayer giving her the answer that answer being Jesus. I still feel so amazed at what God did that night, I remember how scared I had felt when I was moving to intensive care yet through the night all my worry of how ill I was had just washed away. Jesus had that very night come and healed me and saved me and the next day my heart was just so full of joy and there was no reason for me to be feel that way. Other than the peace and love that I felt directly from Jesus, it is a feeling that I often look back on and it still brings deep joy to my heart when I think of that morning.

People often look at the miracles of Jesus and these dramatic on the spot healing that he gave to people suffering with all kinds of afflictions, my own healing was slow and definitely drawn out and is still ongoing but I had no doubt in my heart that Jesus was the reason that I was being healed. I had many days that ended in sheer frustration as my body did not seem to be responding to treatment, but I was getting much stronger and I truly felt the Lords hand upon my life and his loving care for me each day.

That Friday evening I phoned my wife to say goodnight to her and my children, I was missing them all so much it felt like I had at times been cut off from them and I can not tell you how much that hurt. My daughter was only six months old when I had fallen ill and she was now coming up to her first birthday. After talking with my son and having a short time of baby talk with my daughter I chatted with my wife. I had sensed when she answered the phone that she was not happy about something and now she was ready to tell me what it was! She told me that someone from the church had seen her out shopping with the man she had committed adultery with, it was strange as nobody had told me anything about her having been seen with him. Yet here she was telling me all about it, she told me that nothing was going on and that he had been a great support to her while I was in hospital. I could not believe what I was hearing, how was I supposed to take this news. I had told her that she had to break contact with this man and yet here she was out shopping with him. I told her over the phone that there was no way that our marriage could survive with her having a friendship like this, and how could it!

She seemed to think that I should be happy that they were friends that I should have no problems with my wife having a friendship with this man that had in her own words taken advantage of the fact that I was in hospital. She became very angry on the phone and in a fit of anger hung up on me uttering words at me that I can not repeat. I lay there feeling completely helpless and even tried to call her back but she refused to answer her phone, moments later she sent me a text message telling me that our marriage was over. In the text she put a list together of all the things that I had done wrong and basically blamed me for everything, even her adultery. I felt totally broken, the physical pain I suffered each day did not even come close to the pain I now felt in my heart, despite me forgiving her she still stabbed me in the heart. I felt at that time as if she somehow gained pleasure out of hurting me and the next few days went by in a complete blur and I have little memory of them, I just remember feeling so sad and broken and so numb.

The condemnation from my wife had really broken me and it seemed that nothing I did was correct in her eyes, things had always been a struggle before I fell ill and I worked so hard to try and keep our heads above water, working all the overtime I could get, but in truth it did not end just there as often when I arrived home from work my wife was invariably out somewhere with the children and the house was a tip so I would start all over again. It seemed to never cross her mind to clean up and it was down to me to do it and on top of that I was cooking most of the meals. When I brought up the state of the house with her she would just get defensive and tell me I did not know how hard it was for her each day having to look after the children. The roller-coaster I was on with her emotions each day drained me so much and left me feeling exhausted. Yet I loved her so much and would do anything for her or my children. I had worked hard at home trying to make our house nice for her and had when I had the money taken her out to the cinema or for a meal and I tried so hard to make sure we did something nice each month together.

I was not only shattered and broken by my wife ending our marriage with her list of wrongs! But found myself completely confused, I was sure there were things I did wrong and I believe that we don't get everything right. But what hurt me the most was the fact that I was still in hospital and had effectively been charged with all wrong doing and was not in a position to even put things right my health had to come first. I felt as though all the blame was mine, that I had been a bad husband but I could not see how the charges that she had stacked up against were true and they appeared very warped.

I prayed for God to guide me and asked him to reveal to me what I should do, what I should say but God was telling me just to be patient and to keep quiet. Sure enough God proved to be right as on the Monday afternoon my wife phoned me in floods of tears, she asked me if she could come to see me the next day so we could clear the air. She explained to me that she felt that she had been very rash in ending our marriage the way she had and wanted to talk to me face to face. I agreed that it would be good to talk and even arranged with the staff at the hospital for us to have a private room so we could talk in peace. I sat that afternoon and wrote a list of things that were important to me. I set out what I expected of her and number one on my list was that she cut off all ties with this man, I knew that for us to have any hope of rebuilding our marriage that she would have to do that. My list was not extensive and I felt that the things I was expecting of her were not too much for anyone to ask for, but I was not sure how my wife would take to them.

The next morning I prayed that my wife would have the heart to listen to what I had to say and also that I would also have the heart to listen to what she had to say. When she arrived that afternoon I wheeled myself round to the front door to meet her as the room we had been given was near the main entrance, she thanked me for accepting to see her, but I was just glad that she wanted to. She began by asking me to forgive her and asked if I was willing to give her another chance. She explained that she was so stressed out with everything, I sat there and listened before replying. I told her that I was willing to forgive her and give her another chance to sort out the mess. Instead of reading out the list I had made her, I gave it to her to read herself! I told her that the only thing on the list that had to happen was that she ended all contact with this man she had committed adultery with. Everything else I just wanted her to work on and strive to be better at. I also explained that I knew I was not perfect and that I would also strive to do better in the future, my wife took all that I had to say very well and she thanked me for giving our marriage a chance to survive and for forgiving her again. Relief rushed over me and I praised God for his mercy.

PROVERBS 20 VERSE 12, the hearing ear, and the seeing eye, the Lord hath made even both of them.

My wife hugged me and gave me a kiss before having to rush off to pick our son up from school. I received the best news around ten minutes later when my phone buzzed with a text message from my wife. She told me that she was so happy that I had forgiven her and that she was going to put everything into our marriage, I sat there and smiled feeling so relieved and with a new hope in my heart for our future. The last few months had been a real trial not only for me but also for my wife and children, my daughter was still very young so in truth I was not so worried about her, but my son must have really struggled with what had happened to his dad. It certainly had not been easy for any of us but now I felt as though God was truly bringing renewal and although the suffering was hard the hope in my heart was stronger than ever. God was with me in the centre of the storm holding me and giving me the strength to keep on going and my faith was strengthening day by day.

Kosovo 2000

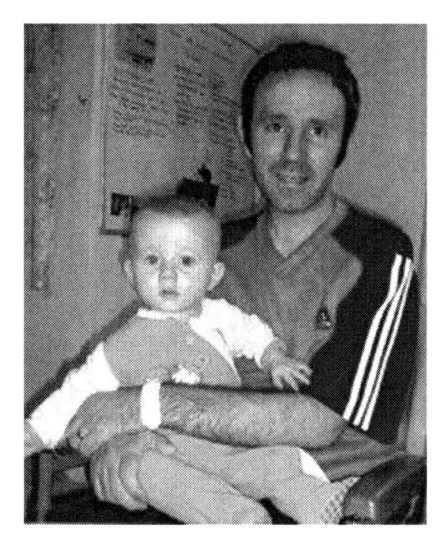

Hospital with my daughter

Home with my mum, David and daughter

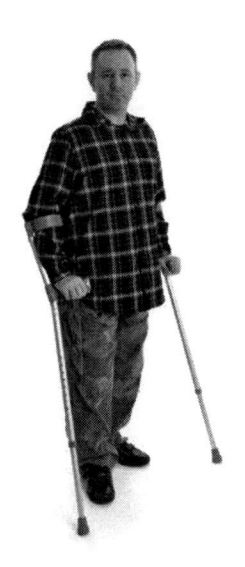

music and back on my feet

Pastor Jim, Billy and Jez

Me in 2012

CHAPTER 7

SUNDAYS ARE FOR GOING OUT

One of the struggles that I had faced during my time in hospital was of letting go of some things, one of those things had been our marital home. Very early on I had been very objectionable to even the thought of moving house and I told those who raised the subject that I loved the house I lived in and that was the end of it. Over the course of the months I spent in hospital my objection to moving house melted away, the truth was I could clearly see now that the house we lived in was just not suitable for me to live in. for one, no matter which way you approached the property you had to contend with steps, and I could quite clearly see that I was not going to be tackling steps for a good while if at all. Two the house did have a problem with damp on the front wall I came to realise that moving back to that house was just not going to be possible. So in early January one evening when my wife had come to see me along with Ruth I had given my consent for my wife to put an application in for a more appropriate house for us to live in. I could sense the relief in my wife that my stubbornness had finally melted away. So with the help of our local social services she went ahead and got an application for us to be re homed with our current landlords.

A few weeks later my wife phoned me from my friend Les's phone, she told me that we had been offered two houses that were already adapted for somebody with disability's. She seemed really excited about one of them as it was situated just across the road from my son's school, she explained that Les and Mary had taken her and the children up to the property to take a look at the house. This house sounded as if it was perfect for us, and it was as though God had purposely chosen this property for us as not only was it where my son went to school, but our church also held our Sunday services in the school building. To find that God would put me so close to the place where we worshipped I knew was no accident, my wife soon handed the phone back to Les after I had given her the go ahead to tell the housing association that we wanted this property. Les began chatting to me about the house but I could tell that he was walking away from it as my wife's voice got quieter, Les told me that once he and his wife had dropped my wife back off at home they were coming to see me. I informed Les that Visiting hours were already in the last hour that was allotted for the evening but he was insistent that he and Mary would pop in to see me as he told me that he needed to talk to me.

I lay there wondering what was so important that he and his wife would feel that they had to see me that evening! By the time they did reach the hospital there was only about fifteen minutes left of visiting time. The pleasantries were as usual, hi Jez how are you etc. Les soon began to explain why they had rushed to come and see me. Something strange had happened earlier that evening when Les and Mary had decided to go and see my wife, whilst out shopping they had seen something and decided to buy it for my daughter whom they are the Godparents of. Les explained that my wife was acting very strangely the whole time they were there and had closed the kitchen door, Mary had been chewing some gum and got up from the sofa just to go and put the gum in the kitchen bin. My wife had practically jumped up and blocked Mary from going into the kitchen and told her that the kitchen bin was full so could she put it in the wheelie bin outside! I have to say it sounded very strange to me, one piece of chewing gum was hardly going to make the bin overflow and fall out all over the floor.

My wife had mentioned to them the two houses that had been offered to us. So Les asked her if she wanted him to take her to view them from the outside and my wife jumped at the idea of going to see them. Further to this also at my house was my son's friend who just happened to be the son of the man my wife had committed adultery with, so my wife asked Les and Mary to take the boys up to their car while she got our daughter in her car seat.

I lay there bewildered at the fact that this man's son was in my house, it meant that my wife was not only still friends with him but completely ignoring the things I had told her just days earlier about cutting off all contact with this man. As Les and Mary waited for my wife to come up from our house, Mary asked his son if he was missing his daddy to which he just nodded his head, but my son replied to the question "well he is not far away is he, he's only in the kitchen". Out of the mouths of babes the truth comes out, it was a huge revelation and it hit me like a sledgehammer. Les and Mary said they were sorry for bringing such bad news but I thanked them for there honesty, the truth for me always mattered and I was not in a position where I could see what was going on for myself. Deception had always been something that I detested and I now knew that my wife was lying to me. I felt that it would now be very interesting to see how she responded to this. Before going that evening Les gave me a piece of scripture and I have to say that it fits perfectly with what was going on,

PROVERBS 27 VERSE 6, Faithful are the wounds of a friend; but the kisses of an enemy are deceitful.

That night I went over it all in my head so many times but the truth was that I was just making myself angry, I hoped beyond all hope that it was just something innocent but I truly felt that it was something very serious! in the end I decided that the best thing for me to do was to get some sleep and just to hold the whole situation with her in my prayers.

I woke next morning and began my day with prayer, I prayed that my wife did truly want our marriage to be saved and also for us to enter back into a loving relationship and during that prayer a thought struck me, maybe from me but maybe from God that perhaps she was just after a new house. That thought cut deep within me and led me to pray to God that he would cut through any lies that were being told to me, all I wanted was the truth and right at that point I have to say that my faith in my wife was completely shattered.

I left it all in Gods hands and decided not to challenge her over this but waited to see if she brought the subject up herself and I did not have to bring it up as the following weekend my wife came to visit me in hospital. She began by telling me that she knew what Les and Mary had told me about. She then went on to tell me that nothing was going on and he had been simply picking his son up as this boy had come for tea. She also explained that when Les and Mary had knocked on the door it had been his idea to go and hide in the kitchen, she added that it had been a silly mistake of hers to allow him to do that. I sat there in my wheelchair musing over my wife's version of the events of that night, and although I was not completely convinced I decided that I would give her the benefit of the doubt on this occasion. I told her that I did not want her anywhere near this man again, my wife though seemed to think that it would be unfair on our son as he and this boy were such good friends. I explained that they were in the same class at school and could see each other there each day, to this my wife said nothing. It all seemed to add up to me that she was somehow unwilling to give this man up but my wife eventually nodded her head in agreement.

Though it had been a hard afternoon in terms of the topic of conversation I did still enjoy seeing them, I loved them all so much and was so determined to get better so I could be a husband and father again, all too soon visiting time was over so I had to say goodbye to them, that was always the hardest part seeing my family go home while I had to remain there in hospital.

I often sat there or lay there in hospital wondering why God was allowing me to go through so much heartache, what was the purpose of all this suffering. God I knew allows such things as he did with Job. Since being in hospital I must have now read the book of Job many times, his suffering was on a level that was so much greater than the suffering I was experiencing. Job had lost everything his children, his wealth and his health but the real attack came when even his own wife turned upon him.

JOB 2 VERSE 9, His wife said to him, "Are you still holding on to your integrity? Curse God and die. The pain of your own wife turning against you is one that I knew only too well, but Jobs response shows the true heart of the man, Verse 10, He replied, "You are talking like a foolish woman. Shall we accept good from God, and not trouble?" in all this, Job did not sin in what he said.

My wife had often come to see me and asked me how I could believe in God when such an awful thing had happened to me, she had on occasions also rubbished any belief in God and said that the bible was just a book that anybody could have written. This showed me that she was greatly troubled by everything that had happened. I so often told her that without God I would not have survived, yes it had been touch and go for a little while, but God had answered prayer and was still doing amazing things. It shocked me that she could not see all that he was doing. How much his hand was upon our lives as he watched over us and cared for us. All of our friends were rallying around and giving her great support, and caring for our family and loving us, she somehow missed the fact that God was giving his love to pour out upon us through our friends, but in her eyes that was not God it was just people doing good deeds. I sometimes sit even now and hope that I could have the same strength as Job had when his wife turned against him, that my words would and could have been full of wisdom, yes I put my whole trust in God. I know that Jesus had saved me and there was a huge reason for him to save me and it was not for me to wallow in self pity, but to be freed of my burdens and live in victory, but self doubt has always been one of my weaknesses.

I now had real doubts that my wife truly wanted our marriage to work and to be fruitful, I felt that when I became ill she had decided that I was going to die anyway so she cut herself off from the pain by moving on with her life. Sure I knew that it must have been extremely painful for her to see her husband cut down the way I had been with my illness, but the greatest shock for her seemed to be that I had survived and was now starting to get better. Every time she came to see me she could focus on her own pain and how our son had been affected by my illness but somehow miss the suffering I was going through, it felt as though my feelings and pain did not matter, everything was about her and the children and how they were suffering. All I asked for was her full support and love, that she was one hundred percent behind me, but in truth I felt all alone and abandoned. It was as though I was a broken toy and it was now time to throw me away, writing this is so hard for me. To open up my heart this way but all I asked for was love and it seemed to be the one thing I was not getting, I was receiving pain and more pain on top of that from my wife.

That same Saturday a group of the men from church were all coming to share an evening with me and were also bringing one of my favourite meals to share too, CURRY!

It was such a blessing to be missing the hospital food, four months of it had really taken its toll and it was so nice to be having something different. So while all the other patients went off to the dining room at five o'clock I sat in my room waiting for my friends who were coming around six. When my friends arrived I was so hungry and the curry smelt so good, the staff had after the evening meals for the other patients gone to the trouble of preparing a table for us all to sit around I felt so blessed by the care and love poured out by them for me and my friends.

In all there was around eight to ten of us sharing that meal together, sharing our lives and enjoying each others company and our faith in Jesus. The evening was one I will never forget as I felt Jesus was among us as we sat and ate. To be surrounded by friends who love you and care for you was so wonderful, as in truth I felt as if the wind and the waves of the storm that was raging around me were getting too strong and that at any time it was going to consume me or completely crush me. But I was left after that evening with a renewed strength in Christ.

After the meal Jim our pastor asked me if it was OK for the men to gather around me so they could pray for me and I welcomed the prayers of my brothers. Their prayers gave me such a lift and after the guys had spent some time praying for me Jim asked if anyone had a piece of scripture that they felt needed to be shared, for a few moments their was silence and Jim then as we were in silence before the Lord asked me if their was anything on my heart that I could share. I had sat there in my wheelchair as the men were gathered around me thinking that one of my friends would share when all the while a piece of scripture was burning in my own heart so when Jim asked me it suddenly dawned on me that God had wanted me to bless the men with this in return.

ISAIAH 35. The whole of Isaiah 35 I felt was calling out to me at that moment as I felt so strongly that it was not only a personal message for me but also a message for the church, but in particular verses eight to ten spoke to me so much about the salvation that we were gaining through our faith in Jesus and in particular the end of verse ten had given me so much hope, They will enter Zion with singing; everlasting joy will crown their heads. Gladness and joy will overtake them, and sorrow and sighing will flee away.

I often still marvel at the way God works things out but often it is just that God has given so many of us the same thoughts and pieces of scripture in our hearts at the same time. Jim was himself amazed at what I shared as it had also been a piece of scripture that was on his heart too, it is often in those moments when you share something like that that you truly realise that it was Gods plan all along, you have to have the faith to trust God and say what God has put in your heart to say. Isaiah 35 is such a special piece of scripture to me as so much of it talks of renewal and the joy and the glory of the Lord, and verse three is particularly apt for me, STRENGHEN THE FEEBLE HANDS, STEADY THE KNEE'S THAT GIVE WAY.

I feel now as though I no longer need to explain just how weak my body was at that time, but I knew that without my faith in Jesus I would have remained bodily weak, without my faith I could never have faced all the trials that I had already come through and I was certain that there was probably more to face. Jesus however was with me all the way and with Christ as my shield and my protector what could man do to me, I knew that it would not be easy to follow Jesus and in fact if we look at scripture again in the gospel of Luke it says in Luke 9 verse 23, if anyone would come after me, he must deny himself and take up his cross daily and follow me.

As that evening with my friends drew to a close their prayers were not only about asking God to continue healing me but they also prayed for my wife and children, that they would have peace during this difficult time and that my wife would take all of her worries and troubles to the Lord. As my friends said farewell that evening, I was left feeling completely loved and blessed, I went to sleep feeling so at peace and for the first time since having fallen ill I had a full nights sleep without waking up in pain at some point.

February began and my legs were by this point really frustrating me, they just were not coming on like the rest of my body. In physio I was working so hard at standing up, and various frames and contraptions were tried and tested out, but I was still at a point where I still needed their help to get stood up and to maintain it once I was stood up.

One evening I even had a little lament of my own, I was asking God why my legs were still refusing to work and why they were showing little signs of recovery, I ended my little moan by asking God to give me more patience. (AMEN TO THAT)

The rest of my exercises were going really well and my arms although very thin and still very weak they were at least now becoming usable again, turning pages in books and writing and general movement of my arms was considerably better than it had been. Every morning when I woke up I would do all of my exercises that were handily all written down on the board next to my bed. My list of exercises would take me almost an hour to get through and some of that time was taken up with me needing to rest as it was very tiring for me, but I was so determined that I would get better and there was no way I was going to just sit there and not put the effort in to recover.

On the fourth of February the physio;s decided that it was time that I tried some car transfers using a banana board, most of you I am sure have never heard of a banana board so I will do my best to describe it. It is basically a board that is shaped like a banana, the board aids a patient in being able to transfer between two different surfaces. I had for a few weeks in physio been using one to transfer between my bed and my wheelchair, although I was not yet allowed to do it with the nursing staff. The board was basically shoved under my left buttock and created a bridge to my wheelchair from my bed. The first few times we had done this I had found it impossible to move and had required the help of the physio's to get me from my bed into my wheelchair and vice versa. Those first few days that I had been working on this had been really frustrating, but I was really determined I would be able to do it. It was during the last week of January that I had finally managed to get across into my wheelchair from my bed without any assistance, that afternoon I had sat there gearing myself up to give it my best shot. Every other time that I had done this I believe that one of the things that had stopped me was fear, fear that I would fall on the floor as I was still quite unstable. So on that afternoon in late January I sat there mustering all my strength with the words of Romans 8 verse 15 ringing in my head, For you did not receive a spirit that makes you a slave again to fear, but you received the spirit of sonship.

So with a mighty heave I put my all into moving on the banana board by myself, for once not worrying if I would fall on the floor or cause injury to myself I just gave it my all and trusted God that he would, 1 give me the strength and 2 catch me if I did become unbalanced, that afternoon I overcame the problems that I had had previously with being able to move myself and although it was not text book banana boarding as Mike put it, I was moving myself in and out of my wheelchair unaided. The grin on my face that afternoon must have been visible from space, once again I was reminded by Jesus that I had to put my faith in him as through faith in Jesus we have strength.

PHILLIPIANS 4 VERSE 13, I can do all things through Christ which strentheneth me.

So when on the fourth of February the physio;s told me that they wanted to try a car transfer I felt really up for the challenge, Mark explained that getting in and out of a car was quite different than getting in and out of my bed as the angles and the car doors make things really different. So that afternoon Mark went and brought his car around for me, at first when Mark put me in place next to the open passenger door of his car I sat there sizing up what I would have to do. After working out the best places to put my hands I got Mark to slide the banana board under my right buttock, I had thought that it might take me a couple of attempts to work out how to get in the car but in fact I found that my first attempt was successful. I then looked out of the car and realised that my wheelchair was quite a bit higher up than the seat I was on. yes I had gotten into the car but could I get back out! After some really tough negotiation on my part of how I was going to get myself up the banana board and back into my wheelchair and having to effectively work against gravity and I finally managed to get myself back in my wheelchair. I was so pleased as this was such a huge step forward for me. my mum had arrived to see me as I was in the process of having another go at getting in and out of Mark's car and I could see that she was impressed with what I was doing. Mark then asked my mum if she could bring her car round so I could have a go at getting in and out of her car as it was most likely that if I was going to go out it would be in my mums car. Once my mum had driven around I had a go at getting in and out of her car and if anything it was slightly easier than Mark's car, I could see how pleased everyone was this was another huge step forwards for me, again my grin must have been huge.

Mark was so pleased with my progress that he not only passed me for doing transfers with the nursing staff in the hospital but also he cleared me to go out on Sundays to spend some time with my family, I felt so elated and could not wait to tell my wife the good news. The feeling of gaining some freedom again and being able to get out for even just one day was wonderful and all this just days after feeling so frustrated about everything and the slow progress that was getting me down.

Jesus had again answered prayer and given me the strength to overcome another hurdle all because I had taken a leap of faith and just trusted him, so often I think that we forget that it is by faith, Hebrews 11 is a great piece of scripture to read on faith, so often we fail and call upon our human strength forgetting that Jesus is our strength, but only if we have faith in him.

CHAPTER 8

BACK IN CHURCH FOR THE FIRST TIME

That Sunday morning two of the nurses were with me bright and early to prepare me for my big adventure out into the world, my mum was picking me up at about nine thirty to take me to church where I was meeting my wife and children, after the service we were all going to my mums for lunch and I was as giddy as schoolboy about the day ahead. I was so excited to be having a full day with my family as I had looked forward to this for so long, what was even better than that was the fact that I would get to do this every Sunday from that day on.

After the early morning call from the nurses and my usual struggle to wash, shave myself and get dressed, I was left with at least an hour and a half to kill before my mum would arrive to take me out. I spent what I thought was a long time in prayer to find that only ten minutes had actually elapsed, so decided to prepare my heart by reading my bible for a little while. I have always found that when I am over eager about something and excited the time running up to the actual event taking place goes so slowly, obviously it does not help that every few minutes I found myself clock watching trying to will the time away.

I also found myself looking out of the window on a frequent basis looking to see if my mum had arrived, even though she was not due yet. As it got closer and closer to nine thirty my feverish excitement grew as did my worry that I would be late as my mum had not arrived yet. It was all so silly the church service did not start until ten thirty and it was only a twenty minute drive to get there, but ever since my days in the armed forces time keeping had remained very important to me, and I still do not like to be late for things even now.

Of course there was nothing to worry about, just moments later my mums car came into view. I put my coat on with the help of a nurse and wheeled myself around to the hospital entrance to actually find my stepfather was the one who was picking me up and taking me to church, David explained that my mum had stayed at home so that she could prepare the dinner for us all. Just the thought of home cooked food made my mouth water, five months of hospital food was quite enough already. Although Jim our church pastor claims to really like institutionalised food, but I was not sure he could continue to enjoy it for as long as I had been eating it.

After I shuffled my way into the car across my banana board and after David had loaded my wheelchair into the car we set off. It was good to get the chance to talk to David as we made our way to church that morning, he told me that most of the bills were now straightened out. I thanked David for all his work on cleaning up the mess we were in financially, it was such a relief to hear that most of it was now sorted out. It gave me such a lift to think that when I eventually would come home for good that I would be doing it from a clean slate. I was excited to be able to tell my wife that we were almost financially straight I really felt that it would be a real source of relief for her as I was sure that she must have been worrying about how we were going to cope with all the debt hanging round our necks like a mill stone.

It was as I had predicted earlier that morning that the drive to church from the hospital would be about a twenty minute drive so we really had arrived with a lot of time to spare. We pulled up outside the building where our church met on Sunday mornings to find that the only other people that had arrived so far were Jim our pastor and the musicians.

David told me that he would be back for us all about twelve thirty. It felt so wonderful to be sat there that morning, Jim came over to speak to me and said how wonderful it was to see me there, all of the hard graft and effort I had put into getting better was beginning to pay off. More of the congregation began to arrive and they were so surprised to see me, nobody had told them that I was going to be there that Sunday morning and I think in all honesty that made it all the more special for them. It was so lovely to see everybody again, I felt so loved as many of them came asked me how I was and gave me a hug, but for me the morning was extra special when the moment my wife and two children arrived. I hugged my wife as best my arms would allow and gave her a kiss. To be there as a family that morning meant so much to me, It seemed like I had waited an eternity for this moment, for us all to be together and not only with my little family but with my church family.

The service began with Jim announcing to the whole congregation that I had come out of hospital to be with them that morning. The whole congregation clapped and cheered and I felt slightly uneasy about being the focus of their joy, I felt like some minor celebrity for a few moments and was brought almost to the point of tears by their love. Jim came over to me with a microphone and asked me if there was anything I wanted to say. The only thing on my heart to say that morning was to tell everybody of my deep gratitude for the love and support they had all poured out for me and my family during my illness. Their truly is no love like the love that God gives to each of us so freely through his son Jesus Christ. After another round of applause the service began with a time of worship I put my all into singing along with everybody else but found that I was often out of breath and it was so tiring for me. It reminded me that my lungs had been so badly affected by my illness and still had a long way to go to be fully recovered. It was really no surprise to me that my breathing was affected by singing as I was aware how tired I was after a physio session, but it did frustrate me that I could not sing that well as it was something I had always loved to do ever since singing with a choir in a church as a boy.

During the service my wife had again asked me how I could forgive her for what she had done, I was saddened to hear her asking this again as it showed me that she had still not been able to move on at all and did not understand the forgiveness that God himself had already given each of us for our sins. I told her again that I was able to forgive her because I loved her and told her that Jesus had taken on all our sins so that we could be forgiven, explaining to her why I was able to forgive her seemed to settle her a little. But all I could think was how troubled she seemed to be and it worried me that she seemed to be so stuck and hung up on what had happened not on what was yet to come.

After the service it was time for a cup of coffee and a biscuit, it was lovely to see my son looking happy and just so special sitting there and being able to chat and laugh with so many friends I had not seen in so long. It was great to hear what had been going on in their lives as they had all heard so much about my illness, it made a really nice change to be able to talk about them although in hindsight most of the little chats I had that Sunday at some point did focus on my illness and how I was doing. It was a chance though to feel like a normal person and not this figure of pain and suffering. Something I felt aware of was that some people felt sorry for me, yet that was not the way I viewed myself. To me it was just the way things were. What was also so lovely though was how many of my friends told me that I had given them such strength and courage and wanted me to know that. I always struggled with that as it was a thought that was alien to me, that I was giving people courage and strength. As I have looked at it deeper over the last few years it was not that it was me directly that was giving anyone courage or strength, but the fact that my faith was completely in Jesus and that he was giving me the strength and that those who talked with me could see that my faith in Jesus was being displayed through my suffering.

One of my friends who I saw that Sunday morning was Karl who had been in South Africa when I had fallen ill, it was great to see him and hear about the ministry he had done in South Africa and he told me that morning he would come to see me in hospital, before he left Manchester again as he was now living on the south coast. The time that morning had flown by and David was soon there to pick us all up and to take us to his house for lunch, so we all crammed ourselves into his car all the while saying our goodbyes as everybody made their way home after the service.

The Sunday roast dinner my mum had made for us was amazing it was like I had never tasted food like it before in my life, and it was so special for me to be spending the afternoon with my family, real quality time! That afternoon my brother and his wife and two children came up to see mum and Dave as well, Paul was still coming to see me every week, but I had not seen Claire and the girls since Christmas day and Claire commented on how much better I looked since the last time she had seen me and told me that she could see the progress herself that my brother was always telling her about. It was so lovely to hear that, I often found that I myself could miss the progress as I was the one living with it every day.

The whole day had flown by and by about four in the afternoon I was beginning to feel uncomfortable as my body grew tired of being sat in my wheelchair, I knew that it was time to be getting back to hospital so David asked Paul if he would help him to get me out of the house, it did mean them lifting me down a couple of steps and I am sure to this day (jokingly) that my brother was doing his best to throw me out of the wheelchair and into the bushes along the way, and his laughter was doing nothing to make me feel like I was in safe hands but thankfully all ended well. I then got myself back into the car and said my goodbye's to everyone and thanked my mum for a lovely day. The only thing that saddened me that day was having to go back to hospital, I had had a taste of life outside of hospital and it was something that tasted so good like sweet honey. On our way we dropped my wife and children at home, I had had such a special day with them and it was sad to say goodbye. My thoughts now more than ever were on when the new house would be ready so that I could start spending whole weekends with them and be a family again. I knew that it was the next big step in getting some normality back in my life.

After dropping my wife and children at home David commented that my wife had barely said a word to me or anyone else all afternoon, to be honest I had been immersing myself in just how wonderful it was to spend all day with them and had not given it much thought. But he was right whenever I or anyone else had spoken to her the conversation had never lasted much longer than a few words. It was as if my wife was some how uncomfortable around my family. At this point I had not told anyone in the family what had happened and I truly did not want my wife to feel that she was being labelled or was not liked by any of them but the truth was there in her actions and something was not right. David went on to tell me that my mum was so worried about me and I could tell from the way that he put it on that trip back to hospital that my mum suspected that my wife had gone off with another man.

I could tell that David was also fishing for answers and I could understand why, there was no two ways about it my wife acted strangely around not only my family but me as well. Again I sat there and had to move the questions aside and tell David that I thought that my wife was just really stressed out and that it could not be easy for her having to look after two young children, it was then that David gave me the killer line. He agreed with me that my wife was probably stressed out but he said that if she is struggling to cope now how much worse will it be when I start coming home for weekends or when I come home for good.

The truth of the matter was that I did not know how she would cope, everything I had seen so far pointed to the fact that she would not. Her anger at times really worried me and she was prone to going off the deep end over the slightest thing. It was certainly something that worried me, but love sometimes can allow you too blot out the worst in a person and to not see clearly maybe where you need to be seeing clearly and I was certainly guilty of that, a quote that I have often used is "Love is blindness".

We arrived back at the hospital and to say I was flagging with exhaustion would be an understatement, it was quite unbelievable just how much energy I had used in one day, I was so drained that I asked Bob who was on duty that Sunday if he would come and assist me getting into bed. David brought my banana board into my room and put it on my bed for me and then said goodbye. I thanked him again for taxiing me around and for a lovely day. Once Bob had helped me get in bed the sheer relief of being able to rest out of the wheelchair was fantastic. Too long sat down could often exhaust me to the point of needing a lie down, wheelchairs do enhance your freedom to get out and live more normally but they also do get uncomfortable to be in after being in them for so long.

The second week of February began with much the same routine for me, physio, physio and more physio! I was good with routine though and I suppose that all goes back to my time in the armed forces where every day was very regimented. I also liked routine as it meant I could focus my day better. One thing that I had taken to doing was going to check the board at weekends and every evening to find out what time I had therapy, the board was there to inform the patients and staff about therapy sessions. On the Tuesday of that week my wife called to tell me that she was coming the next day to see me with the children, my wife seemed really fed up though on the phone and it appeared to me that she was really beating herself up over what she had done, the pain was very clear in her voice and one thing she said that evening was, how could all this have happened to us and that it was not fair. After her call I felt awful, I felt as though I had somehow let her down by being ill, I knew it was not my fault but that did not change how I felt about it and in truth I did not know what to do. The best source of comfort I had was my bible and again I turned to Gods word to find comfort, I prayed to God that my wife would turn to him to find comfort. I opened my bible in the book of psalms and was blown away by what I read, God always seems to know exactly what we need and when we need it, he always brings comfort to those who seek his love and compassion and he always gives generously.

PSALM 147 VERSES 3 TO 5, He healeth the broken in heart, and bindeth up their wounds, he telleth the number of stars, he calleth them all by their names, great is our Lord and of great power: his understanding is infinite.

That same Wednesday my dad was also visiting me, he was travelling up on the train from London that morning. So I was really pleased that my wife was coming with the children as I was sure it had been some time since he had seen his grandchildren. My elder brother Paul also visited that afternoon and my mum. So I really did have a room full of visitors, It was so lovely to see everybody. My wife still seemed very stressed though and I could see that she seemed none too pleased about something, she and the children had not been there that long when my wife's stress suddenly turned to anger. She shouted at our son for nothing and grabbed him while he was in tears and forced him to put his coat on and without even a goodbye she stormed off home with the children. I sat there feeling very embarrassed and so shocked at her behaviour and I hung my head in shame. We were all left feeling very shocked at what had just happened and none of us said much for a few minutes. I had seen my wife angry before but this was an anger that came out of nowhere and their was no reason for it. It hurt me so much to see my wife behave like that it would have not have been so bad if it had only been me that had to witness it, but to have that happen in front of my family was awful.

My dad was beside himself with worry about it, as he was leaving to go back to London he chatted with Paul on the way and the main point that my brother brought up was the fact that it was obviously a very stressful time for my wife, having her husband ill and having to look after two little children and she had not actually hit our son just forcefully frog marched him home, yes she had grabbed him but nothing more.

The next day I was having a home visit with the occupational and physio departments from hospital, this was so that they could evaluate what adaptations would be required for me to be able to spend time at home and eventually leave hospital all together, my wife was meeting us at the new house with a member of the housing association who would open up the property for us. Upon arrival at the new home I felt nervous about seeing my wife after the way she had behaved the day before, but she came walking down the footpath smiling and waving to me, it was as though the day before had never happened. She chatted pleasantly with me and the two members of staff from the therapy department as we waited for the housing officer to come and open up the house. I sat there almost bewildered by just how twenty four hours later it was like talking to a completely different woman than she had been the day before. Finally the housing officer arrived, the house already had good access for me as the property had a concrete ramp that went down to the side door, and inside although much work was still needed to be done it seemed as though everything was going to be just right.

A stair lift was already fitted and although I could not yet use it or get on it when we tried I knew that in a few short months with the way my strength was returning that it would not be a problem. All in all I was very pleased with the house and the therapy team who had come with me seemed to be enthusiastic about it too, the housing officer told me that she would get the contractors to begin all the work that needed doing as soon as possible. I could not help but praise God for his wonderful hand in getting us a house like this, not only was the house perfect for us but the location was fantastic as it was so close to our sons school and our church too, I knew Gods hand had been at play in getting us a house this good and I knew that this house was a gift from God.

My wife's change in character inside just one day worried me, it actually left me feeling very confused. A thought that went round and round in my head was that I wondered if the change was only because my wife wanted a new house, that it had nothing to do with being with me. I worried that once she got her hands on this house I would be history and she would again end our marriage. I was not the only person who was picking up on this train of thought, Ruth had dropped in on her way home from work one evening that week and said exactly the same thing that had been going through my head. She told me to make sure that when the day came that we would sign for the house that I would also be there to sign my name on to the tenancy. This was not an issue for me and I told Ruth that there was no way that I was going to leave the house with just my wife's name on the tenancy. She told me to let her know when the house was being signed for and she would take me to do that that day. Ruth's willingness to give up her own time and just give of herself like this truly tells a story about the type of person she is, a humble servant! I praise God for friends like Ruth they are truly one in a million.

Worry aside I was really excited about our new home as I truly saw it as a chance for us as a family to have a new start in a new home, it was as though God was giving us every opportunity to have the old replaced by the new. God is a master of renewal, that much I knew for myself. My life in many ways because of my illness had been completely transformed

Faith—Through the storm

from one where I lived with what I would personally call paper thin Christianity. I had for too long thought that it was all about me, never thinking that God had a plan but that the fact that I believed in God was all that mattered and that I could live my life in the world doing the things of the world and then on Sundays be this Christian man and I had lived by my own strength not Gods. What is true is that every day even when I was at work I would pray to God, but all too often they were personal prayers for myself or my family seldom ever were they for anybody else or for the situations that were happening around the world. Yet I had witnessed first hand the barbaric hand that man puts upon other man when I had served as a soldier in the army. Kosovo was an eye opener into a world that many westerners only hear about in the news, To see a ninety year old woman who had carried what possessions she could for well over a hundred miles just to escape persecution was very humbling. I only went to the refugee camp once during my time out there but to see whole family's now living in make shift tents, reliant upon charities like the red cross is something that I will never forget.

    I have said earlier that God was at the potters wheel, shaping and moulding me into a new man and the man I was being shaped into was so much the better for it, my prayers no longer seemed hollow or misplaced and God had revealed so much about himself through everything I was going through that I felt so alive with his love pouring into my life every day. God was using my experiences and deepening my relationship with him through all the suffering I was going through. Teaching me and nurturing me into this new man, there is no greater love than knowing the love that God has for each of us and feeling his love and compassion. Jesus had been with me right from the start of my illness, because he knew the things that I was going to face and knew how painful they were going to be and who better is there to be by your side than Jesus when it comes to suffering. Jesus knew suffering very well, better than any other! Jesus wanted me to feel his love from the start so that I would trust in him and as I look at the things I had already come through I knew that I would not have managed it had it not been for the love that Jesus poured out into my life. It was not so much that Jesus walked by my side but that he carried me, there was not two sets of footprints in the sand but just one set at that time. I could clearly see Gods hand in everything and every day I see his hand in so much more than I ever have before. God not only comes to you himself to show his love but through others to express that love through them. The amount of love that had been poured out at times overwhelmed me to the point of tears, so much does God love us that he sent his one and only son into the world not to condemn the world, but to save the world through him.

The one thing that comes to mind through this is FAITH! God wants us to lean upon him through all of our troubles and cares, God wants us to take everything to him not just the little bit that we invariably do. Ultimately he wants us to trust him! That whatever the situation may be, God will work it out for the best not us. Before my illness so much of my life revolved around what I could do, not what God could do. I did so many things in my human strength never thinking that there was one who when I gave it to him and let him be my strength, would work it all out for the better. The truth was that I made a mess of many things and to this day I believe that God was left with a situation where he had to do something extremely radical to sort the mess out that I had made. God took away my human strength leaving me in a position where the only thing I had left was him, I had to trust him no matter what I was going through and it is all about FAITH.

I wrote one of my songs around this time during my time in hospital and I think that it is fitting to share the words from that song with you here in the book, the song comes from Psalm 119 verse 105, your word is a lamp unto my feet, and a light unto my path. Also it comes from James 1 verse 2, Consider it pure joy, my brothers whenever you face trials of many kinds. This piece of scripture from James I added later as it seemed to fit so well and God gave it too me one night but I will tell you of that later.

WALKING IN THE LIGHT

No matter what I'm going through
I know you'll be there
No matter how long the road
I'm walking with you
Your word is a lamp unto my feet
Each step I take
I take with you

Chorus
> Walking in the light you give give
> You are holy
> Walking in your light
> Beautiful one (repeat)

Verse 2
> When life's down in the gutter
> Still I will call to you
> The roads end I can not see
> But I'm walking with you
> Your glory fills the sky Lord
> And I'm on the road
> You heal my soul, Jesus

To put our whole faith in complete abandonment of ourselves is to many such a scary thing to do, and it was scary for me too. God however wants humble men and women who look to serve first before their own self needs and that whatever we are going through we take it all to him, and let him work it out. So many times during my time in hospital I could have chosen to try and work my problems out myself and not trust God. Yet God had had to in the first place take me to a place where I would completely trust him as I had nothing else left. One thing I have learnt about faith and prayer is that we do not always get what we expect from God yet get everything we had asked for.

The physical jumps I had made to get to the point where I was now able to go out at weekends was a massive step forward for me, it gave me such a boost at just the time I had really needed it! Gods timing is always perfect when I look at how desperate things were the night I was taken up to intensive care, and then look at what happened through all the faithful prayer! All thorough my time in hospital prayer was being answered by God. Every trial I had faced so far, every piece of love poured out upon my family, God had been at the centre of it all graciously giving, pouring himself out upon me and my family. It led me to a place where my faith was growing stronger day by day and my love for Jesus just deepening day by day. Every morning when I woke I invariably woke with a song in my heart and would just begin singing that song as my worship to Jesus, I am not sure what the staff made of this or if they could hear me through the closed door but my heart could not be kept quiet, though I was suffering much I was also being so deeply blessed that love and joy just poured forth from me. JESUS, YOU ARE THE KING!

CHAPTER 9

MORE HEARTACHE

The week that I had just had left me feeling so positive and as the next week of my recovery began I had more cause to feel positive. On the Tuesday of that week I found yet again I was able to do something that I had failed to do every time I had tried before, every morning the nursing staff would come in and sit the head rest up on my bed so that I could have breakfast and a wash. Once all done I decided that I would listen to some music whilst still on my bed, as too long in the wheelchair could have adverse effects to strength later in the day. As I have mentioned earlier it was my usual routine every morning to go through the exercises that were written on my board. Not that I really needed to read through them any more as I knew them all so well. One of the exercises the physio's had given me was to try and sit forwards from the back rest of my bed. Up until that morning it had just all been about switching the muscles on and then relaxing them again without me moving anywhere but that morning was to be very different. As I did the exercise I felt my back come away from the bed behind me and I sat myself forward, excitement overtook me and I had to do it again and again just to be sure I had really done it. At times all the hard effort did seem to be for nothing as my body did not seem to match up to the sheer effort that I put into my recovery, but when new things like this happened it truly did remind me how much it was all worth it. I gained great encouragement when something new like this happened.

I had a physio session later on that day and when I told them what I had managed to do they wanted to see it for themselves, so my bed was set up for me and I shuffled across on my banana board to get back on to my bed. I rested a moment gathering my strength then showed the physio's my new found talent. This meant that they felt I was ready for new exercises to help strengthen those muscles even further. That was it with me, I was always opening myself up for more hard work to do and the truth was that I actually revelled in it and enjoyed the challenge that getting stronger brought.

Later that evening when I phoned my wife to tell her that I had made another jump forwards physically I thought that she would be pleased, but she seemed to not even care that I was getting stronger. It was as though nothing that I did mattered to her all she did was pass the phone to my children so that I could say goodnight to them and then after a few words she told me she was tired and that was that. She did not even tell me that she loved me or seem to register the fact that I loved her. Yes she said she was tired but I was tired every day, in fact I was shattered every day. My illness really took it out of me and everything I did was a real effort just to do. Her attitudes towards me and the coldness in her voice left me feeling so sad and confused. She blew hot and cold and I got a sinking feeling that she simply did not care for me any more, it was like she had simply fallen out of love with me and that hurt so much.

That weekend when I went out on the Sunday one of my friends from church picked me up, between the church and my family they had come to an arrangement of every other week either my family picking me up or somebody from church. My friends in church had also arranged that when it was them who were going to pick me up a member from church would invite me, my wife and children for dinner. The love being poured out again just left me in awe of how merciful, how loving and caring God is. For many of my friends from church I was sure that they found great joy in being able to express their love to me and my family in this way, it was something that they could do for us and in many ways they wanted to give their love, as for some people they did not know what to do or say. so to be able to express their love through inviting us to their homes for dinner I was sure for them was one way they could. The feeling that I got from all this was that this was their gift from God to us as a family.

I felt so humbled by all the love being poured out for us, it was being given so richly by everybody and I felt guilty that I could not give anything back, but I found that assumption of mine was wrong. Many of our friends would tell me how blessed they felt to have us round for lunch and they often marvelled at the work that God was doing in my life and told me that they were drawing such strength from what I was going through, they would tell me that my faith in God inspired them and gave them hope. In truth I felt that their was nothing marvellous that I was doing, nothing that was spectacular! I have said earlier that I knew that what was spectacular was the work that God was doing, and God despite all my weakness and suffering was now using me to give people courage and strength. He was able to show people his grace and hand at work through me as a living testament and that really humbled me to find God using me in this way. No matter what the situation may be if you allow God into your life and allow him to work through you, amazing things will happen.

It always makes me laugh, the things that God uses to make a point to people, as humans we often look upon strong things to draw strength from! In Hollywood all of the heroes have rippling muscles and are masters of using that strength to bring down a corrupt evil empire, dodging bullets along the way. I don't recall many or any films where the tough guy who was going to save everyone was the weediest person you could imagine ever coming across. Who barely looked strong enough to even be able to save even himself, and then we have God! It seems to me that God loves to ignore all the rippling muscle men or women and gets to work by using the most weak individuals he can find and doing amazing things through them, we only have to look at scripture and we can see this pattern leaping of off the pages of our bibles at us.

It totally amazes me the way he does it because often and I count myself in with this, the weak person can not explain it or understand how or why God uses them, I had no idea that I was such an inspiration to my friends, it came as a complete shock to hear my friends say these things to me.

2 CORINTHIANS 12 VERSE 10, Therefore I take pleasure in infirmities, in reproaches, in necessities, in persecutions, in distresses for Christ's sake; for when I am weak them I am strong.

Jim our pastor was quite aware of all the suffering that we as a family were going through and an idea of his during that time looked like such a good one, he had suggested that me and my wife write a letter each week to one another. The basis of the idea being that we rekindle our love through the letters. The idea reminded me of being a service man and writing home to a girl that I had been dating at the time, it was a place where you could be yourself and I really thought that it was a wonderful idea for me and my wife to be able to share the things that we loved about each other, to regain that intimacy that had been ripped away by my illness and her adultery. I was really up for doing everything we could to save our marriage from the fire. My wife came to see me one evening with Billy one of our friends from church and when I told her about Jim's idea, she told me that Jim had mentioned it to her as well and she also thought that it was a good idea. What pleased me even more was the fact that my wife said that she would send the first letter, everything up to that point to me had suggested that my wife did not want to try to even sort out our marriage so to hear my wife being so enthusiastic about this really gave me hope.

My wife's letter arrived later that week along with a beautiful card, the card was lovely and she had written such lovely things in it about what the children had been up to and how proud they all were with how well I was doing. I then excitedly opened the letter. The letter though brought me back down to earth with a bump, this was no love letter. Hatred seemed to pour of the pages that she had written, every little thing that I did wrong in her eyes was written down. She had even listed things that with me being in hospital I had no control over, she ended the letter without even a hint of love and there had been none in the whole letter, but with the words "if you change your ways I will change mine". It cut me so deeply I felt as though a division of infantry men could do me less harm to me than my wife was doing right at that time. There was so much in the letter that was just not true and I felt so deflated, it was like my wife had a knife in my side that she was twisting ever deeper into me.

That afternoon after my therapy sessions I sat in my wheelchair under the window in my room and wrote a letter back to my wife, I felt that I was under such an attack that I ended up using half of the letter just defending myself and trying to get my wife to see reason. I began however by telling my wife how much I loved her and instead of using empty arguments I explained to her how much I had always had put into our marriage. Never in my life had I had to write such a hard letter and I prayed that my letter would only show her how much I had always put into our marriage and how much I loved her and the children.

A few days later my wife came to see me in hospital, she told me that she had received my letter, Ruth had brought her to see me this time and she gave us some time alone. My wife was scathing in her response to my letter, she said that all I was interested in was money as it was one of the things that I went on about in my letter to her. I sat there in my hospital bed and told her "yes, I worked hard but it was to provide for her and the children" my words though were not being heard though in letter or face to face. My wife accused me of keeping money for myself and then told me she had seen my wage slips so she knew how much money I had been earning before I became ill. I was so saddened and shocked at what she was saying to me, every week my whole wage was being eaten by paying the bills and feeding us as a family. Yet my wife could only see the figures written down on my wage slip and from there accuse me of greed and of making my family suffer. Nothing I said seemed to even register with her, I may as well have been talking to a wall and in all honesty I sat there in my bed willing the clock to move faster so that visiting time would be over. I was so glad when it finally was, but even then my wife had a parting shot at me her final words to me that evening were "I don't know why you bothered working anyway, if you are on benefits you get everything paid for you, you are better off".

It seemed unreal to me, was that truly what she had expected from me all the years we had been together that I should have stayed at home and not worked and relied upon state handouts. Did she really want a layabout for a husband, I had always worked so hard to provide for my family but now I had a good idea of the kind of man she had wanted me to be. The next weekend was awful, my wife had continued being horrible to me on the Saturday and on the Sunday I just hid all the pain from everyone at church and in all reality I could not wait to get back to hospital so that I could have some peace. The stress of it all was really getting to me and at times I was having real problems getting to sleep. Some days I was so drained and I really struggled with my therapy, I was living under a cloud of depression but I did everything I could to try and hide it. My mum knew that there was something wrong and often tried to get me to open up, but I flatly refused to to tell her what was eating away at me. The reality of the situation was this, that even I felt my marriage was in a coffin and it was just waiting for somebody to come along and nail in the last few nails to seal its death and I did not want to be the one who finished it off, but it was causing me such heartache that I did not know how long I could go on hiding the truth from people.

Though the pain was hard that I was having to deal with I did have the best help anyone can have, Jesus! Spending time in prayer and reading my bible always gave me such comfort from all that I was going through and so often particularly after my wife had cut me with her acid tongue, Jesus would come and give me his peace and his comfort. I needed that peace and love and comfort again just days later. It was still only the middle of February and I was about to receive yet another body blow from my wife, she phoned me and at first all seemed fine, but suddenly in a fit of rage she ended our marriage again. She shouted at me over the phone and just said it was over, that she did not want to be with me any more. I could no longer handle the pressure of all the pain that I was suffering and called for a nurse to come and see me, I sat there and told her everything that was going on. She listened and seemed shocked to hear what I had been putting up with and advised me that it would be a good idea for me to have some counselling. She explained that it would be good for me and it would be good for the therapists as it would explain to them why I did not seem to be getting better at the rate they would have expected. I had never thought about it that way but it seemed to make sense to me that all the suffering I was going through was affecting my ability and my determination to get better. The next day my mum came to visit me and I could no longer hide the pain from her, I told my mum that my wife had ended our marriage and told her everything that had gone on. My mums first words were "I knew it", I needed more than ever to hear words of comfort and my mum did her best to comfort me but it was only later that day when I opened my bible that I truly found words that gave me comfort.

ROMANS 5 VERSES 1-2, Therefore being justified by faith, we have peace with God through our Lord Jesus Christ. By whom also we have access by faith into this grace wherein we stand, and rejoice in hope of the glory of God.

Without my faith I truly did not know where I would be, how I had held myself together this long under the weight of all that I was going through was only down to the fact that my faith in Jesus and my trust was completely in him. All the suffering I was going through did not shake my trust and faith, I do not say that to boast about myself but to tell you that we all have to let go and put our every needs and hopes in Christ alone. It was wonderful to know that whenever I cast all my worries and pain unto Christ he would in turn give me such peace and hope. Christ was not only at work in healing my body but also in my heart and my soul, he was doing a much deeper work in me than I could ever imagine and I thank him every day for the healing he was giving me.

CHAPTER 10

A NEW HOME

March 2009 began with more problems, my wife had phoned me telling me that she was broke and had no money to get nappies for our daughter, I had no money being in hospital and was not sure what I could do but before I could tell her that I would ring David to see if he could get some nappies for her she hung up on me. I thought that maybe the line had just gotten cut off as the signal could sometimes be very bad in the hospital, so I went and found a good place for signal strength and tried to ring her back. Her phone just rang and rang and after a couple of attempts to get through the next time I tried to ring her the phone was switched off. I was trying my best to get better and do what I could for my family yet when I tried to help it became impossible to do so. Later that day I got an angry voice mail message from her telling me that she had sold my electric guitar as I was not willing to support her and the children. I felt so helpless, the pain and accusations that were being thrown at me hurt so much and I felt as though I was now being punished for not being able to provide for my family. My faith in God was the only thing that was seeing me through what I was having to put up with, and yet again God gave me scripture that spoke directly to my heart and soothed me from what I was going through.

JOB 12 VERSES 13-16, With him is wisdom and strength, he hath counsel and understanding. Behold, he breaketh down, and it cannot be built again: he shutteth up a man, and there can be no opening. Behold he withholdeth the waters, and they dry up: also he sendeth them out and they overturn the earth. With him is strength and wisdom: the deceived and the deceiver are his.

I did not know where my wife was getting counsel from, but I knew it was not from God. Verse 16 seemed poignant to me. I felt that she was being deceived by somebody perhaps this man that she had been seeing, So often we think we have to go in all guns blazing into a situation, and yet I find that so often God wants us to do the exact opposite and just to let him deal with it. I found the book of Job to be of such comfort to me and there are so many pieces of scripture in that one book alone that spoke to me through all of my distress, Job was a man with cast iron faith in God, in chapter 13 verse 15 Job says to his friends, though he slay me, yet I will hope in him. I was finding this out for myself in what was going on in my life, despite all of the constant suffering I knew where my salvation lay, JESUS! That first week in March I spent a lot of my spare time in prayer for my wife, she had drifted so far away from me and from God and I truly wanted her to turn around from where she was headed.

That weekend my prayers were answered, the Sunday when I went out my wife had agreed to bring the children to church so that I could see them. She arrived as we had begun to sing the first hymn, I hugged my son and had a cuddle with my daughter and it was so special to have them there with me that morning. As we were singing songs of praise to God my wife began weeping upon my shoulder, all of her anguish and pain came flooding out, I put my arm around her and told her how much I loved her, she replied "but how can you after all I have done, you should hate me". The earthly me probably did hate her for all the misery she had caused me, but the fire burning in me was the fire of God. His compassion, his forgiveness and his grace! And his grace is enough, who was I not to forgive. I know I am saying that again but God's forgiveness is eternal and he is willing to forgive anyone of their transgressions, Jesus himself had taken upon himself the sin of all mankind so that we could have a relationship with the father. Jesus paid the ultimate price for us because of Gods love for us.

My mum was not convinced that I was making the right decision in giving my wife another chance, However I felt that she deserved that chance. That evening I lay everything before God and put it all upon the alter, putting my complete trust and faith in him alone. The feeling of sheer relief that came from letting God take all my burdens was just wonderful, I felt so much more positive and resting in the Lords comfort was amazing. Just two days later talking to my wife on the phone she told me that she had picked up her bible again after months of ignoring it, the change in her in just a few days seemed remarkable and afterwards I wept in praise to God. I prayed more than ever that now she would understand the truth and be freed from her guilt as she read her bible, I was so pleased that she was seeking God again.

On the physical front my upper body continued to improve and I could just about lift both of my arms above my head by the middle of March, I also learnt another new trick that month. I had for the last few weeks been doing an exercise where I lay on my bed on my side with my legs hanging over the edge of the bed, and then using my arms to push myself up off my side to sit myself up on the edge of the bed. Each week I got a little closer to managing to do this without the help of a physio, so when late on in the month I managed to do it unaided I was really pleased. The effort just to do that alone left me exhausted but exhilarated. Muscle fatigue and exhaustion were truly one of the biggest things that I faced daily in my attempts to get better, often I would find that I myself was willing to carry on with therapy sessions and do more only to find that my body was not. That in itself left me some days very frustrated but if there is one thing that God has taught me while I was ill, it was patience, and boy oh boy did I need plenty of it.

My legs finally were showing signs of some recovery, I was now whilst lying on my bed just about able to move them up and down with my heels resting on the bed. All of the movement was coming from my thighs as below my knee's in both legs I still had no muscle activity and that was still a great concern for me. My doctor explained that with Guillain-Barre syndrome the nerves have to regrow and unfortunately they do not grow very fast, she told that she had been looking into the illness and from what she could see, recovery from this illness varied so much from one patient to the next. One thing she said was that in some sufferers it is like the nerves just go to sleep and then reawaken. She told me that patients who have that experience with the illness tend to recover far quicker, some within a couple of months. She then went on to explain about the other experience that patients have with the illness. She explained that the longer the time needed to recover was, the more it tied in with nerves dying and then having to regrow. Patients who have this kind of recovery she said can often end up with some nerve damage, My doctor seemed to think that my nerves were having to regrow and that there was a chance of me having some nerve damage now. I was so aware of how slow my recovery had been and this news that it was a good possibility that I could have nerve damage was hard to take. However if anything this did not blunt my determination it gave me the heart to fight on and continue trusting God with whatever lay ahead.

I had been having counselling sessions each week now for a couple of weeks and one of the things that I really wanted was some space to sort my head out in, since arriving in the hospital I had had no fewer than four room mates and the constant merry go round of getting used to a new person to share your room with was beginning to drive me crazy. So during one of my counselling sessions I told my counsellor that it would really help if I was moved to one of the one man rooms that the ward had. At the time of asking the ward did not have any of theses rooms available but one of the wards sisters came to see me one afternoon and told me that I would be kept in mind in the event of one becoming available.

Counselling did little to help me get over all the pain and anguish I was feeling but it was a good process to be involved in if only so that the staff knew I was dealing with far more than just my illness. The truth of the matter is that I had the best counsellor anyone can imagine having, Jesus! I know for a fact that Jesus was daily unburdening me from all that I was going through and giving me freedom from it all.

I knew that the counsellor obviously cared, but I can safely say that I was very surprised at what little did go on in those sessions other than for my counsellor to ask me after I had spoken about what was bothering me "how do you feel about that". That seemed to be the typed response, I often wondered if she was sat there with her clip board in front of her and their was a list of things on it that all said answer with "how do you feel about that". It sounds as though I am having a go at the professionalism of the NHS counselling services, in truth I am not I am merely stating that Jesus for me and for anyone else is the best counsellor you can have. He will come and speak truth into your life and bring you comfort like no other can "he has amazing grace". It is something that no human can emulate or get close to, without Jesus I truly felt I would have been lost.

March was a month of progress like no other, I had been using my banana board now for some time and late on in March I had a physio assessment where Mark passed me for getting in and out of bed on my own using my banana board, the freedom this gave me was immense. It now meant that I could get out of bed in the mornings have a wash and a shave, get myself dressed and just get on with my day! Gaining more independence was so wonderful. The first day that it was all down to me to get myself up was one of the scariest days I had had, up until then I had always had somebody there with me helping me as I got myself up so to suddenly be flying solo took a lot of courage. I soon got used to it though and it became just second nature.

Over the months I had gotten to know many new friends, one new friend I had made during that time was Peter, his wife Jane had brought my children to see me for the first time while I was still in Hope hospital. I had met Peter on a few occasions before my illness as they went to the Anglican church on the estate where I lived. Les and Peter had suggested that they come down to the hospital every Friday evening and that the three of us would do a bible study. Les told me to pick a book of the bible for us to study. Jim had been to see me in early March and suggested that I read the book of Hosea so that was the book that I chose to study. Those Friday evenings were such a blessing to me, I had not had the opportunity to have a bible study since falling ill and it was wonderful to be able to do that again. I said that Jesus is the best counsellor you can ever have, well he does not just counsel directly into your own heart. He sends those very special people of his whom have his love is at the centre of their hearts to also minister healing and counselling to you in times of trouble. I so often find myself in complete awe of the way God works everything out for the good, how he helps those in need, his grace just blows me over. I felt so blessed to have such good friends, and that is no mistake or accident God always knows what we need and gives so graciously.

At the end of March my wife phoned me to tell me that she had received a letter from our housing association telling us that our new house was ready for us to sign for. The date we were to sign for the house was Thursday the second of April, the news that finally we were going to have our new house gave me yet another boost. I called Ruth that evening to tell her the good news, Ruth told me that she would come and pick me up and take me on the day. All that week I waited excitedly for Thursday to come. Early that Thursday morning Ruth arrived to pick me up and take me to the housing office. As we were on our way there I could tell that something was bothering Ruth and so I asked her what was wrong? She said that she was not sure that she should tell me as it was about my wife. I told Ruth that whatever it was it was better that I know the truth. She told me that she hated to be the bearer of bad news, but told me that one of our other friends from church had seen my wife earlier in the week walking up to school to drop my son off in the morning with this man whom she had committed adultery with. When my wife spotted our friend from church they had quickly parted company and walked on opposite sides of the road. Ruth apologised for bringing me more bad news, but I told her that I was thankful to her for her honesty and that I would rather know the truth.

One of Ruth's favourite pieces of scripture she shared with me that morning, and it is so fitting. JOHN 8 VERSE 32, And ye shall know the truth, and the truth shall make you free.

It seemed to me that the trust that I gave my wife was constantly being shattered, we soon arrived at the housing office and for a few minutes we sat in Ruth's car and prayed about everything that was being hidden by my wife to be revealed, I also asked God for guidance and that I was doing the right thing. My wife arrived minutes after we had arrived, I could see that she was in a bad mood but I had no idea why. Once we were in the office alone that was when my wife's bad mood was explained. Almost right away after the housing officer had gone off to photocopy the tenancy agreement my wife started firing accusations at me, "so was this Ruth's idea you being here to sign for the house"? "No I replied, actually my idea". It seemed crazy to me that my wife had felt that I would not want to come and be there and sign for our new home. So after what Ruth had told me that morning I really felt I must challenge her about her being seen with this man again.

My wife again had what was in her eyes a cast iron excuse, she very defensively said "I can't help it if he is walking the same way to school as me and we were not together". The housing officer came back into the room, I tentatively signed the tenancy all the while in the back of my mind was the thought that my wife was lying to me. We were handed the keys and told that we had two weeks to move into the property, but one of the things that I was very aware of was the fact that that was Easter weekend so I asked for an extra week to move in which we were granted. We decided that we would all go down to the house and have a look at it. We entered the property and I have to say that I was very pleased with the work that the contractors had done, I sat there in my wheelchair in the living room feeling really pleased that at least we had a home that I could start coming home to at weekends now. By the time me and Ruth set off back to the hospital my wife's mood seemed to have changed and she even gave me a kiss before we set off. On the way back to the hospital I explained to Ruth what my wife had told me about her and this man being seen together. Ruth said though that it was a lie and she completely trusted the person who had told her what they had seen. Ruth went on to say that when my wife noticed that they had been seen together it was like the parting of the red sea the way they moved apart and that this man does not even live in the same area of the estate. So why would he be walking his son to school from the direction of my home. As I evaluated what I had been told the only thing that seemed to make sense to me was that this man and his son must have stayed over for the night in my home, but I had no concrete evidence that that had happened I just knew that whatever did happen from this point on I had to proceed with caution and lots of prayer.

Later that afternoon as I continued to think about how my wife was obviously telling lies I felt relieved that I had been there that morning to sign for the house. If I had not been there the house could have been hers alone and as we were getting this house based on my disabilities I felt that would have been truly wrong. That Friday when Les and Peter came to continue our bible study Les told me that he would decorate the home for us, I felt so blessed and so loved by all our friends, so many people had put so much into helping us and still that help was not drying up. I gave Les a cheque to buy the paint and wall paper that he would need and told him to get in contact with my wife so that he could have a key for the house. The Lords blessings just continued to pour out and I am amazed at how much God was blessing us as a family.

PSALM 29 VERSE 11, The Lord will give strength unto his people; the Lord will bless his people with peace.

CHAPTER 11

MOVING IN AND MOVING ON

The first weekend of April was my daughters first birthday, it saddened me to think that I had missed out on the last six months of her development and she had grown so much in that time. My mum had put together a little birthday cake and family celebration for us at her house on the Sunday afternoon after church. The church service that morning had been fantastic, Jim's message that morning had been about seeing Gods love through pain and that in itself was something I could certainly relate to.

ROMANS 5 VERSE 5, And hope maketh not ashamed; because the love of God is shed abroad in our hearts by the holy ghost which is given unto us.

I have to say that although at times my own suffering has been great and the pain has seemed unbearable, through those sufferings Gods love has been pouring out into my life and I have had some of the most blessed times I have experienced. I find that God comes so close and ministers his love directly into our hearts all we have to do is receive that love and stand in faith.

It was a lovely party for my daughter, the afternoon was so special and spending time with my daughter and family meant so much to me. We were joined that afternoon by my elder brother Paul and his wife and children and it was lovely to see them as well and spend time just chatting to them. All in all the time me and my wife were able to spend together always felt too short but it was still special. Money continued to be a problem between me and my wife, but on the side of all the debt that had mounted up while I was ill things were a lot better. My stepfather had sorted everything out and had even brokered a deal with my car finance company for him to buy my car off of them, David had done really well to sort out all the mess. Their was still one loose end that my dad was trying to sort out and he was hitting all kinds of stumbling stones but he continued to work at it looking for a solution. My biggest worry was that my wife had learned nothing from all of the hardships we had had to go through because of debt, I now felt that we as a family had that clean slate to work from which could only help us as a family. We now had enough money to be able to pay for the move to our new home and decorate the house, again I could not help but praise God for the mercy and provision that he gave us and as it says in psalm 68, O God you provided for the poor.

When we had been offered this new home the money to move in to this property was just not there and being in a situation where I could not work to earn the money necessary for the move had left me wondering how we would cope and pay for it. God always though has the answers and about a week before the move to our new home I began to receive benefit from the state that replaced my sick pay that I had been, the timing was perfect and was so needed at that time but that's just the thing with God his timing is always perfect. Les had been busy decorating the new home and Peter and Jane had gone with my wife to buy flooring for our living room and everything was in place so that we could move in to our new house. Money was not the only thing that God provided though he provided man power for that move, so many of our friends in church gave up a Saturday to help us move into and that humbled me so much.

Everything was falling into place just perfectly and my wife was really keen for me to spend my first night at home on the day we were moving in. I myself was a little apprehensive as it would mean me not having nurses on call when I might need them through the night but in all honesty I very rarely ever needed the nurses through the night any more. I was given the all clear by my doctor and therapy department at the hospital to stay at home that weekend and I truly felt as though my life was getting back on track. David's words also replayed through my mind when he had told me about how my mum and he worried about how my wife would cope with me at home as well. I was going to get my first taster of how she might cope with having me at home and having to care for me as well as the children and only now would I find out.

On the Saturday morning of our move day Ruth came and picked me up from the hospital to take me to the new home. I was wheeled into the property and got my first look at the place, Les and his boys had done a fantastic job on the place and the living room looked lovely. The new flooring had also only just been laid down the day before and I was so grateful to everybody for their hard work at turning our home into one that could be lived in. it was so lovely being there in my new home, the only thing that pained me was that I could not be of any help to anyone as they beavered away bringing our furniture in to the house and all our appliances. The guys and girls were working hard at both ends, some at our old house helping tidy everything up and some at the new house moving things around and making our new home beautiful. As lunch time rapidly approached I gave Ruth some money that I had set aside so that I could buy everybody a chip shop dinner. Peter and Jane had also chipped in to help us move and peter and I had spent some time sat in the living room chatting that morning it was so nice to sit there and have company, I told Peter about the music that the Lord was laying in my heart to sing and that I felt he wanted me to record it. Not only did Peter know what equipment I would need but he could also get it all for me and I was totally amazed. I was very excited about finding this out and once again it seemed that God was giving me even more blessings but also further confirmation of what I was doing musically and that God wanted me to do it.

Carpets were getting laid upstairs and furniture was being arranged downstairs and I sat there feeling like a spare wheel. We sent a message to the guys at the old house that dinner was on its way and they all arrived just in time so that we could all share it together, the move had gone very smoothly and there was not much left to do after lunch. Everyone had worked so hard and as we were finishing our dinner we had a group photo taken so that it could be put in the church magazine! God seemed to constantly be putting all the pieces of the jigsaw right into place I could not help but see his hand at work, through my recovery, the sorting of our finances, the new home and everybody's help. The constant blessings we were receiving were amazing and now to find that Peter could help with sorting out the things that I would need to be able to record the music and songs just amazed me even further. I always felt so overwhelmed by what God was doing despite the situations that I found myself in but one thing was for sure God loved me and my family immensely.

By around four in the afternoon all the work was done, I was so grateful for what everybody had done in helping us to move, Les's daughter had been looking after the children for us and when they arrived I was so excited as this would be the first night that I was going to spend with them in six months. Knowing that from this point on I would be able to spend every weekend with them at home left me feeling so happy, I was having to sleep on a bed downstairs as the stair lift was still a bit of a struggle for me but I was determined as ever that I was going to overcome this obstacle as it was probably one of the obstacles that was preventing me from coming home full stop. The truth was though that I did not care one bit, to be back together as a family each weekend and to be able to build our marriage was what mattered to me and this was the first step of what I was sure were many to come.

Early that first evening Peter and Jane called at our house unexpectedly and they came bearing a gift, they had been out and bought us a new dinner set. It was so thoughtful of them to bless us like that, I asked them if they wanted to stay and have a cup of coffee but they declined telling us to enjoy our time together alone. About nine that evening both me and my wife were shattered and we decided it was time we got some sleep, I was so tired that I nearly forgot to take my evening med's. I woke early the next morning as was the norm for me and it was not long before my wife and daughter joined me, my son had obviously had a very busy day the day before but when he did surface the look of pure joy on his face to see me there that morning was so wonderful. I had missed moments like that and it really made me well up in sheer joy. My wife had coped wonderfully that weekend and over the next few weeks that was a trend that continued, the fact that she seemed to take it all in her stride gave me so much hope and she was as calm as I had ever seen her which filled me with hope.

Back in hospital physical improvements continued to be painfully slow but as usual it was steady, from the waist up my body was doing fairly well. I now had full range of movement in both my arms and although I suffered with pain in both arms and cases of dropping things, they were much stronger than they had been. One thing that I was very good at was inventing new exercises to help with strength and I found that using elastic bands on my fingers to improve their resistance was paying dividends for me. My legs still lagged way behind, and my lower legs still had no movement in the muscles, every morning I used theraband which is like a big elastic band just coloured differently for the level of resistance each band gives you to exercise my legs I would hook the theraband over my feet and then using my thigh muscles I would push against it whilst holding onto the two ends of the band. I was also now able to do mini sit ups using the theraband hooked over my feet so my strength was slowly returning, but my legs still frustrated me greatly.

ROMANS 5 VERSES 3 AND 4, But we glory in tribulations also: knowing that tribulation worketh patience; and patience, experience; and experience, hope.

Hope does not disappoint us as it says in Romans in the next verse, I knew and still know that God would continue healing my broken body my trust was and still is fully in him but we can only do that by perseverance. Be that perseverance in sufferings be it in prayer or in our daily lives with any given situation we find ourselves in. God wants those that are willing to fight to the last to hold on to him and completely give themselves over to him in faith and perseverance, I often think of Joseph when I think of perseverance. Sold as a slave by his brothers and on top of that all of the things he had to endure, thrown in prison by his master. Yet through all of the sufferings he endured he persevered through them all and honoured God in every way with his life, even fighting temptation to lie with his masters wife.

My weekends out had so far been lovely but all that was about change, the last weekend of May my wife was in the worst mood I had seen her in. Her anger and attitudes towards things were awful and she was really worrying me, I even drew a picture in my diary of myself with steam emitting from my ears I was so stressed. I felt that we needed a miracle for our marriage to survive now, I tried to show my wife love and affection but nothing seemed to work and if anything everything that I did say just made her anger worse. I was so glad when my mum picked me up that Sunday evening to take me back to hospital.

I began the first day of June with prayer for my wife, the awful weekend that I had just experienced I did not want to experience again, my wife's constant changes in her moods confused me so much and I longed for stability in our relationship.

A new development in my treatment began that first week of June, which saw me once a week going the half a mile down the road to the main hospital in Stockport. Hydrotherapy! Therapy in a pool, doing exercises in the water made them a little easier and I found that I was able to move my limbs far easier than I was on dry land. It was exhilarating to be able to move my limbs so freely and I was now hooked on the sessions that I had every week. Of course it was not just about being in the pool I had to do a lot of hard work whilst I was there, and after about thirty minutes I was often very tired. But even after just two sessions I could tell that the hydrotherapy was having a massive effect on my strength and was helping me make huge improvements over a much shorter time frame.

In June I had yet another team meeting with my doctor and therapy teams. My mum and stepfather came along and although my wife said that she would be there she did not turn up. Mark my physio told my doctor that he wanted another couple of months to work with me as he could already see the massive improvements I had made since beginning hydrotherapy and that was really encouraging for me, it seemed I was now on a upward curve and every week I was now making good progress. I had also in early June moved into one of the one man rooms in the hospital so now had the peace that I had wanted. Later the same day as my team meeting I wheeled myself up to a wooden frame that I had in my room and grabbed hold of the handles of the frame. Mark had put the frame in my room and given me licence to have a go at standing up on my own, so every day for the last few weeks I had had a go at it. I sat there a few moments composing myself and gathering strength and then just put all my effort into attempting to stand up, their was a little bit of twisting in fact probably a lot of twisting but suddenly I was stood up! I was amazed and overjoyed to have managed to do this on my own. The stand itself probably only lasted five to ten seconds and when I tried to do it again I found that I could not due to fatigue. I praised God for what I had managed to do and as the rest of the week went on it just got easier and easier to do, Mark was so impressed when I told him I had stood up and he came down to my room to see me perform this little miracle. I could see that he was very pleased with my new found abilities.

Every year our church and Mottram evangelical church have a church in the park service, although for the last two years we had had to do church in the church as the weather had been so bad. This year though I sat there in my wheelchair basking in glorious sunshine listening to the sermon and watching all the various groups who performed things that they had prepared for the afternoon. Spending the afternoon in the park with my wife and children was so lovely, I never seemed to get enough fresh air being stuck indoors most of the time, and it was lovely to see so many of our friends from Mottram who had all been praying for me and our family during my illness. Afterwards as I got back into Ruth's car to make the trip back home and then back to hospital I was completely shattered and really I struggled to get back into her car. It seemed to take more effort than usual, but I would not have missed this day for anything and watching my children enjoy the slides and swings made it extra special for me. Just as everything in the park was packed away their was a loud clap of thunder and the heavens began to open up. God had kept the rain and bad weather back just long enough for us to bring our outdoor event to a close, the loud clap of thunder was like God saying "right you have had your fun now go home".

That weekend Peter gave me a laptop computer, I was completely amazed at being given it and asked him if he wanted any money for it but Peter told me no as it had been given to him. He also had been busy getting all the equipment together that I would need to record music with and gave me it all that weekend too, he had put a recording studio onto the computer for me to play with and to record the songs the Lord was laying in my heart and I felt so blessed to be in a position where I could begin to record the music.

Everything that I felt the Lord was asking me to do was being put in place and I am always amazed at how God brings things together. Musically I was doing much better with the guitar too, and I was getting to grips with chords and chord changes through songs. I had spent a lot of time tinkering in hospital with my guitar often sounding fairly awful but I was now at a point where simple chord changes were possible. I think back to the day when my guitar was brought into hospital for me and I could only just get a note out of it, my prayer back then was that I would be given the gift of music again by the Lord and he honoured that prayer. Having all the tools to start recording the songs the lord had given me filled my heart with a deep joy.

In 1 Timothy 6 verse 17 it says, charge them that are rich in this world, that they not be highminded, nor trust in uncertain riches, but in the living God, who giveth us richly all things to enjoy.

CHAPTER 12

THE LORD IS MY STRENGTH

PSALM 28 VERSE 7, The Lord is my strength and my shield; my heart trusted in him, and I am helped: therefore my heart greatly rejoiceth; and with my song will I praise him.

Physio sessions in hospital continued with slow but steady results and with the addition of the hydrotherapy sessions I was making good progress, and by early July I was able to do around six stands during a physio session so from going from the one stand that I could initially do I had made great progress. I felt that the progress I was now making was in no small part down to the work I was doing in hydrotherapy sessions. Their was one negative result however that I did get in early July, during one physio session my lower legs were tested by trying to stimulate the nerves. The idea was that with the aid of this small machine they used to do this test my foot should jump upwards with the current being sent to the muscle to stimulate it, but even on full strength both of my legs or feet in this case did not move one bit. I could see from the reaction on the physio's face that this was not a normal reaction and she felt that my feet should have moved a little at least. I asked her what this meant and she answered me honestly! This basically meant that their was no nerve regeneration so far going on below my knee's. Although this was a set back for me it did not stop me in my fight to get better, just a couple of days later I saw one of the consultants on the ward and I told him about how my nerves were not yet seeming to recover below the knee's. He explained that with Guillain-Barre syndrome it was quite possible that this test would fail to give the results normally expected with it. What the doctor told me put my mind at rest, although I was well aware that I was now getting to a point where the longer my nerves did not regenerate the less chance their was of them doing so fully. In some ways the results of that test gave me more strength and determination and I knew that God would be my strength always and I was not worried about the result. I knew that God would heal me if it was his will to do so but I also felt that it could be that God would leave me with some disabilities, as a way of reminding me of all that I had been through. Jacob had been left with a limp after fighting with God as a way of reminding him of his struggle and I now found myself in a place where I could embrace whatever God did with my life.

At home life was really hard with my wife, her moods changed as often as the wind did. A week into July she rang me to tell me she did not want me to come home that weekend as she needed a break. I listened to her words and tried to plead with her but she just told me I was being selfish and was only thinking of myself. I felt so unloved, the idea that she needed a break from me really hurt, I was after all her husband. At every turn I had stood by her, at every opportunity I had forgiven her and on top of all that I was dealing with an illness that had cut me down and left me paralysed. Some days I woke up and longed just to get up and go for a run or just to do something that I chose to do, yet every day was filled with physical struggles and physical pain, but for me I met those things head on. God had not given me a spirit of defeat and never have I had a spirit of defeat I was victorious over all of my struggles but not in my own strength but in Christ. God kept me going through all of my difficult times and one piece of scripture he gave me during all of these troubles was 2 Corinthians 1 verse 3, Blessed be God, even the father of our Lord Jesus Christ, the father of mercies, and the God of all comfort.

That weekend Ruth picked me up from hospital on the Sunday morning so that I could go to church I felt so saddened to be in a position where we were back to this and my thoughts about my marriage all ended in resignation, the only one who could answer what was going on for me and what to do was God and I sought his counsel on this more than ever. Late on during the service my wife turned up with our children, their were so few of us that morning that we had all sat on one side of the church with the other half of the chairs empty. So when my wife turned up I thought that she might come and sit next to me but no, she sat on the opposite side of the room, as far away from everybody as she could.

She could not have made herself look more like an alien if she had tried to, after the service she said "I thought I would bring the children to see you while you were here". I thanked her for her gesture of letting me see them but one thing that stood out for me was that it was not that she herself wanted to see me. All too soon we had to leave so after just thirty minutes with my children I had to say goodbye to them, I went to tell my wife that I still loved her but she just said that she had to go Their was no show of any love for me at all, she just left. I had no idea what was going on but I felt so alone, one of the couples in our church graciously asked me to dinner that Sunday and I could tell that they were worried about what was going on.

A week later my wife was a completely different and she was even pleasant with me, to say my head was mixed up would be the biggest understatement of the year. The signals I was getting from her were so mixed that I truly did not know what to do or where in fact our marriage was heading. My wife seemed to have a real capacity to be nice one minute and then horrible the next, but by the end of a July their was yet another weekend where I was not going home. This time because my son was not well with suspected swine flu that was going around, so that weekend I had another of being with friends from church and it seemed that everybody wanted to entertain me. First off was Peter and Jane's where I had a light lunch and then we all went to Les and Mary's for food and streamed church from across the pond in New York, And then later I went to Phil and Ruth's. I had an amazing day out but by the time I got back to hospital I was completely shattered but so grateful for all the love that everybody had poured out for me that day.

The very next day I got a phone call from Ruth asking if she could come in around half five to see me, visiting hours did not start till six so I had to clear it with the nurses. So when the evening meal trolley arrived I hurriedly ate my dinner and then under arm power made my way down to the foyer area to wait for Ruth. It was a beautiful sunny day so when Ruth arrived we decided to go out into the garden at the back of the hospital. We sat and chatted for a few minutes, but I knew Ruth well enough by now that for her to ring me and ask to come and see me their must be a reason for it. So I asked her what was bothering her, again Ruth told me that she was not sure if she should tell me. I explained to her that I was far happier knowing the truth than for it to be hidden from me. Whatever it was it was obviously weighing heavy on her heart. Ruth then told me that my wife had been seen out shopping with this man again just the week before. Ruth gave her apologies for bringing me more bad news but again I thanked her, without the church and their eyes I would have been in many ways walking blindly over what was going on and again I am drawn to say "you shall know the truth, and the truth shall set you free". Their was more for me to hear on top of that though, the first time I had not gone home because my wife had needed a break they had also been seen together. All this news of what my wife was trying to hide from me started me thinking and another piece of the jigsaw just fell into place.

When my wife had phoned me to see if I could get someone to babysit our children while she went out to get the medicine when my son was poorly, I had phoned one of the young girls in our church to see if she would babysit, she had seemed apprehensive on the phone about agreeing to look after the children and now I felt I knew why. Me and Ruth had a time of prayer and prayed into the piece of scripture about knowing the truth and it setting you free I asked God to reveal the truth to me and to uncover any lies that I was being told, nothing else mattered now I wanted the truth. All I felt was that my wife was spinning a web of lies all the time and it had to be broken.

After Ruth had gone I rang my friend who was the father of the young girl who had babysat for us that day and it turned out that he and his wife were already on their way to see me. When they arrived they explained that their daughter had been told what my wife was doing while I was in hospital and that was why she had been so apprehensive on the phone. I thanked them for being so honest with me and told them that if their daughter felt that because of what my wife was doing she could not babysit then that was fine with me.

Over that week, Jim my pastor visited me in hospital as did Peter and Jane. Having to tell them what had been revealed to me that week was really hard but they all told me that they would pray into the situation. Just a week later the truth was revealed, God brought all the lies out into the open. That weekend I again did not go home as now it was my wife's turn to be ill and my daughter too, so on the Sunday my son was brought to church from our house by Les who picked him up for me. He spent the day with me at my mum's and during a chat with him about his mum being poorly he innocently told me that his mum was being looked after by this man, further to that he told me that this man stayed over at our house in mummy's bed. As the saying goes, out of the mouths of babes you will find the truth.

Later that day when I was back at hospital I knew I could not continue any further with trying to hold our marriage together, it seemed to me that every time I gave my wife an opportunity to get things straight, she took that as another opportunity to carry on seeing this man. I felt so foolish, all the time she had secretly been continuing this affair and my trust in her was completely gone now. A couple of days later I received a text from my wife telling me that she knew what our son had told me but that he was just mistaken and that he had told me about something that had happened ages ago. but what my son had told me coupled with what Ruth had revealed to me seemed to be painting a very different picture from the one that she was telling me. God had also given me a gift of insight, when I had prayed to him that the lies and that the truth would be revealed to me he gave me the ability to see the tales being told to me for what they were, and I could clearly see that this was just another smoke screen. When I saw Ruth that week and I told her what my son had revealed to me she was deeply saddened but now at least I knew the truth. Despite the heart wrenching truth of it all God was more than ever bringing me comfort, I found that spending quiet times in prayer or just listening for Gods voice really did wonders for me in helping me get through all that I was going through. I think it is true to say that what God wants us to do is to go to him with all of our problems, to surrender our burdens at the foot of the cross so that he can then heal us of all our pain and I know the comfort that is Jesus and his comfort is better than any I have ever received in the world.

That following weekend I told my wife that I could no longer continue with our marriage because of what she was doing and God was telling me it was finished in his sight. I told her of all the things that I knew about and that she and this man had been seen together on many occasions. To my surprise she did not deny any of it and she had no lies to tell me right to my face. Later on that day I heard her on the phone talking to her boyfriend, after her chat with him she came down to tell me that nothing was going on and that people must be seeing things. I could barely believe it she still had the bare faced cheek to lie to me, one thing I was sure she had forgotten about was the fact that I had the ears of a bat and had practically heard what she said to her boyfriend on the phone word for word. She went on to tell me that they were just good friends and that was all it was. It was just lies as well and I told her that it changed nothing as I had clearly told her that she had to break all contact with this man for our marriage to even have a chance of surviving. On realising that I was not being fooled and knowing herself that she was unwilling to give this man up she changed tack. She told me that if that was the case then we should tell the church that we had come to a mutual agreement about splitting up. She also told me that she wanted no pressure off anyone in the church to stay with me. To my surprise my wife told me that she still wanted me to come home at weekends so that I could spend time with the children, although the situation was not ideal in us having to share the house at weekends it did make sense for the children's sake and it pleased me that I was still going to be able to have those weekends with my children.

As for who would end up living in the house I knew that was down to my social worker and care team from the hospital. But the fact that the house was already adapted for my needs as a disabled man, and all the feed back I was getting from them was that my wife would have to move out because of that. It again showed me how much God was caring for me and looking after my needs, all the while he had been working away in the background sorting out one thing after another and I can say again that I felt really blessed.

CHAPTER 13

GOING HOME

All the stress of what was going on had left me feeling really worn out and it was all so intense that I was having real difficulty sleeping which in turn was leaving me struggling some days with my physio. A few days after our split my wife turned aggressor again and was pointing the finger at people in our church for gossiping about her, the truth was though that the very person she was accusing did not even know what was going on. Only a handful of our friends were in the loop and I knew that none of them would be spreading gossip. Finishing my marriage had been the hardest thing I had ever had to do, my own parents split when I was about eleven years old and it was something that I did not want my children to have to go through. God however was with me constantly and his comfort was such a blessing to me. During one early morning prayer time God really spoke to me over my marriage as I sat there quietly listening for his voice, God told me that my marriage was in complete sin because of what my wife was doing, he then told me that I had to end my marriage as it was in no way honouring him to keep this marriage alive. I had always believed up until then that divorce was wrong yet here I was being told by God to divorce my wife, to end our marriage. God continued to speak to me as he could sense the unease within me over what he was telling me, and told me to read in the gospel of Matthew chapter nineteen. As I began reading this piece of scripture I have to say that I felt more condemnation over what God was telling me to do than freedom but it was when I read verse nine that I understood why God had told me to read it. Matthew 19 verse 9, I tell you you that anyone who divorces his wife, except for marital unfaithfulness, and marries another woman commits adultery.

Telling my friends that week that my marriage was over was very hard for me to do, I was not sure how they would take the news. God however however had prepared their hearts. Jim my pastor at church took what I told him and understood why it had come to this, he told me that under the circumstances he felt that I was doing the right thing. One thing he did tell me before going that day was not to close the door on my wife as in time she may eventually turn away from her sin and realise what she was throwing away. My time in counselling came to an end at the end of July as well and I have to say that although the lady who I saw each week was a lovely person and obviously very caring the sessions had little if any bearing on how I felt, as I have said earlier I had the best counsellor I could imagine having, Jesus! Jesus gave his counselling for free as well, and will counsel all who come to him with their problems, fears and worries. The worlds ways are, well how can I put this, well a world away from how God deals with things and I can safely say that his ways are priceless and better. I know that without my faith and without Jesus I could never have gotten through everything that I have gotten through.

August began and I began to see real improvements with my strength, Mark my physio was so impressed with my progress that he felt it was time to try something new and I soon realised what he had in mind. I had wheeled myself down to the physio gym and transferred myself onto one of the plinths when Mark came into the room pushing a walking frame that was on wheels. This was no normal looking frame at the top of it it had a horseshoe shaped pad with two handles at the front, Mark showed me how I would have to use this piece of equipment. The horseshoe pad was for your arms to rest upon so that with your hands holding onto the handles at the front you could support yourself with your upper body whilst trying to move forwards.

This would have to be done from my wheelchair but with my body only being good from very specific heights to stand up an extra cushion was going to be needed. So with an extra cushion in the wheelchair I transferred back into my wheelchair for my physio session. I wheeled myself into the middle of the room and Mark pushed the frame in front of me. The sheer effort it took just to stand up was immense but I managed it on my own without help from the assistant who was working with Mark that afternoon, Mark was suitably impressed with that in itself but never mind Mark being impressed I was over the moon with what I had just achieved. Mark then asked me to see if I could move the frame forwards myself, it was something I had not done before and from going from just simple standing work to a position where it was now a case of trying to move was quite a scary prospect. I heaved my upper body forwards which in turn moved the frame forwards, but it was then that I hit my first snag. Although I could move the frame forwards I could not maintain that forwards movement and the frame would then go back to where I had started from. All the effort I had just exerted left me needing a short rest so I sat down in my wheelchair for a few moments, the physio;s then came up with an idea, on the back wheels of the frame it had brakes, their idea was that if they put the brakes on it might stop the frame from moving backwards after I had pushed it forwards. I was game for anything that would mean me having a chance of actually being able to move the frame. Although I was worried that with the brakes on it would stop me from being able to move the frame at all but as Mark pointed out the brakes were not brilliant so it might just be that they gave only just enough resistance.

So I again got myself up and prepared myself to give it my all to try and move forwards, at first I only gave the same shove that I had the first time round and this time I went nowhere. I stood there feeling a little annoyed it seemed as though I was not going to be able to do it, I was sure that one of the problems that I faced right at that moment was fear. I was scared that if I did give it my all the result would be that I would end up falling on the floor. As these thoughts went through my mind suddenly the fear of failure was even worse than the fear of falling on the floor, Mark looked at me and I was sure he was about to say "well we gave it a go".

PHILIPPIANS 4 VERSE 13, I can do all things through Christ which strengtheneth me. I felt like giving out a war cry as those words from Philippians went through my head, with a surge of strength I gave a loud grunt and thrust myself forward in abandonment of fear, the frame moved forwards! This time it did not move back, the brakes being on had worked! I stepped forward into the frame and gave it another hefty shove, again it moved forwards! That afternoon I took about eight steps using that frame and I had learned another valuable lesson, when we say we can't, Jesus always says we can because he will give us the strength to overcome. Fear itself can be paralysing and in many ways I felt like a baby again, from the very beginning of my recovery I had had to learn how to do everything again, I had had to relearn it all and this was a training course like no other.

After seeing Mark one minute about to give up on me walking to watching his face have a look of complete joy as he saw his student (patient) take his first steps was a wonderful thing to see, I was even more exhausted than usual and straight after the session I needed a lie down but I was so elated. I knew that this was another huge step forwards in my recovery and nothing was going to stop me now. Over the rest of August and the rest of my time in hospital walking with this frame became a daily exercise in physio, eventually I progressed from that frame to a zimmer frame and my walking got steadily better. I continued to have sessions over at the hydro pool and those sessions really helped me gain more strength as my body continued to improve. One piece of scripture that became a really big piece of scripture for me and one that I still look to over and over again is, ISAIAH 40 VERSE 31, But they that wait upon the Lord shall renew their strength; they shall mount up with wings as eagles; they shall run, and not be weary; and they shall walk, and not be faint.

Talking with my social care team over the marriage break up it was clear from them that the house that we had moved into was going to be mine and not my wife's. My wife was not happy with this when I told her over the phone, but I have to say that I was very pleased that this decision had been taken out of my hands. My wife did seem to understand and immediately put an application in at the housing to be re homed. I prayed to God that she would be swiftly found somewhere to live, it was not that I hated her just that she had put me through so much over the last year that I found being with her very difficult. I continued to pray that splitting up with her was the right thing to do but God continued to speak with me on this and every time he had a piece of scripture that continued to confirm what he was telling me and one of those pieces of scripture was Ephesians 6 verses 10 and 11, Finally my brethren, be strong in the Lord, and in the power of his might. Put on the whole armour of God, that ye may be able to stand against the wiles of the devil.

More than ever God was telling me that I must trust him completely over what was going on and that I must stand firm over the temptation to just give in and allow my marriage to continue, God himself was calling it completely sinful. What was most disturbing during this time was the fact that my wife was still denying that she was seeing this man, yet time and time again she stumbled and the real truth was there to be seen. She tried very hard to hide what was going on but the one problem she now faced was that because of Gods grace and light I could see all the lies for what they were and what was really going on. It seemed unbelievable to me that she could still lie to me right to my face over it. One weekend when I had gone home my wife had taken my children out for the afternoon, for weeks I had been desperate to try and use my stair lift so I could get upstairs it was one of the things that was holding me back from coming home permanently and that particular weekend I managed it. I took a ride to the top of the stairs to find that my upstairs wheelchair was close by so I reached for it and pulled it closer, I transferred into it and then took myself for a little tour upstairs. It was something that I had never seen in this house and it was lovely to see my sons bedroom and my daughters I finally took a look at what would eventually become my bedroom, as I looked in around the door I spotted a red book on the floor. I recognised the book as it was one I had used while I was doing kids church, I reached down to and picked it up to take a look at over the teaching notes in it that I had made. To my horror I found that my notes were gone and that my wife had turned it into a diary. I should not have looked at what she had written but all the truth of her deceit was there in ink on the pages, I only looked over a few pages but the hatred that poured from them towards me and how she was full of love for this man was as plain as day for me. It truly saddened me to see the things that were truly in her heart. What was worse for me was the fact that she was still denying the truth, yet now I had seen it for myself.

In September I had visitors I had not seen in a long time, one Wednesday afternoon Barry and Lisa came to see me. The last time I had seen either of them was the day I left Hope hospital in Salford, and that was in the November of the previous year. Barry had been in and out of hospital over the last few months and they had really been through a tough time, Barry was still in high spirits though and we had a good laugh together that afternoon. Strange as it may seem but looking back to the time when we were both very seriously ill was quite hilarious, the going's on of our daily lives on that ward almost brought me to tears of laughter. It was great to catch up with them and Barry told me before he left that he and Lisa would come back to see me soon and maybe even take me out to lunch one day.

A couple of days later Jim my pastor came to visit me we chatted at length about what was happening and over what to do from this point on.

My wife had made it quite clear that she did not want any hassle off of anybody and wanted to be left alone to get on with her life. So we sat there that afternoon and prayed over it all, as we did one of the physio;s popped in to see me to give me a message. The message at the time I received it shook me to the core, I was being discharged from hospital on the second of October!

That meant that I only had two more weeks left in hospital, Jim looked a little sheepish and told me that he and Michael one of the church's other elders had prayed just that morning that I would not have to spend too much longer in hospital and that I would come home soon. Well God always knows best and although the news of my discharge date did fill me with dread, I knew that God would not have answered those prayers unless it was what was right in his sight. Jim almost fell over himself to apologise for praying for that but in truth it was just another huge step on the way to getting my life back. I may not have liked the idea that I was going to have to go home and live with an unfaithful woman, but God always knows what is right and his timing is always perfect.

God had been clear all along about how my marriage was in complete sin and how he wanted me to end it. I myself was almost daily now ringing the housing association to try and get my wife's housing application moved forward and they eventually agreed to have an officer come and see me at home the week after I was discharged from hospital. Strangely my wife seemed pleased when I told her the news of my discharge date from hospital, so often she would do or say things that completely confused me!

Those last two weeks in hospital flew by, I had spent one week shy of a whole year in hospital and in many ways all the staff and even the irritating buzzers going off all the time seemed like home at times. I had made some great friends and had gotten to know so many very caring people along the way so when it was time to say goodbye to them all it was very difficult to do. My mum had baked a cake for everybody, actually two! One for the nurses and one for the therapy staff and it was lovely to see them all getting excited over a cake. The staff all told me that I must come back to see them and I promised them that I would. Travelling home that Friday afternoon leaving hospital for the last time my mum let me in on a little secret, my wife had arranged a little home coming party for me with our friends from church. I sat there again a little bemused by this show of affection from her and don't get me wrong it was a lovely thing of her to do, but strangely I felt a dread in the pit of my stomach at the thought of having to pretend in front of some of our friends that all was rosy between me and my wife. The party was though lovely and it was special to be home and to know that I was not going to be going back to hospital on the Sunday, I was so pleased as I could now truly begin building a close relationship with my children again and that was very special.

So many friends came to welcome me home that Friday afternoon and it was lovely to again feel their love being poured out for me and my family that day. Being home for good for the first few days seemed somehow surreal, my wife continued to try and hide what she was doing even to the point of going upstairs to make phone calls and the longer we spent in the same house the more ridiculous her behaviour became. It seemed that to me my wife had from the first moment I became ill, just given up on me and nothing had changed now I was home. Their were days where she could be so nice but then in a moment she could turn really nasty and ruin those days, but I was also very blessed to see my children every day and loved being around them all the time. Seeing my son so happy that his dad was home and just hearing him tell me about his day at school was so lovely. My daughter had gotten into a routine of every morning coming downstairs to jump all over me and my bed, but in truth I really loved it, it was so special and every day I praise God for saving me so that I could have these moments with my children. The pain of the last year was not gone but I had a hope now to cling on to and a desire to be the man God wanted me to be.

CHAPTER 14

NEW BEGINNINGS

My meeting with the housing officer went very well, up until that meeting they had been reluctant to move my wife as they simply did not understand the situation. Just hours later the housing phoned my wife and offered her a house, I was completely amazed at the speed at which this offer came through but then when I thought about how quickly God had answered Jim and Michael's prayer for me to come home I knew that God was in it. As there is no mountain too high for our Lord to move. The strangest thing was that my wife had been offered our old house back and that in itself made me chuckle a little. Through all of the last year I had remained loyal to my wife and had at every turn given her opportunity after opportunity to get herself straight so that we could work at our marriage.

Yet every time I did she seemed to see that as a green light to continue hurting me and to continue her affair and only when God had told me that enough was enough had I finally told her that I could not continue with our marriage any more. Yet here was a piece of scripture being played out before my own eyes, my wife had been shown the promised land and yet all she wanted to do was go back to Egypt. Egypt in this little story being our old house, she was running away back into slavery. My wife accepted the housing's offer but there was one small snag with it, as the house needed quite a bit of work to get it ready for living in as a tenant who had lived there had damaged the property, so the house needed some repairs before my wife could move back in.

Friends continued to show their love and support for me and visited me at home. Peter and Jane began visiting me every Friday evening and their love and support was fantastic, and just having them there to pray with me or to chat about the general things going down in my life was in so many ways such a huge life line for me. We have all grown so much in our walks with Christ through this and it has been lovely to pray for them as well and see the results of those prayers. I was now also seeing Peter and Billy on a Tuesday morning for us to get together and play music. Peter had told me when I was still in hospital that he felt that the Lord was telling him that he was to come and practice with me, so when I came home it was one of the things that me Peter and Billy began doing on a Tuesday morning. These mornings have been great fun as we have shared our time together making music for the Lord and just a joyful noise, many of the songs that I have written have had their first try outs in a band situation on those Tuesday mornings. I know that I have been blessed greatly by their input into the songs I have written, one thing that I always feel is central to any Christian walk is to share our lives together lovingly and joyfully. Ruth continues to input into my life, as well as so many other people in the church. I can safely say that having people who you can trust with all the inner pain and the deepest pain of your heart and know that they will pray for you is a wonderful thing and I do believe that that is not just a one way street, as much as people prayed for me and still do I always feel that I must pray for them too.

My wife was not pleased that so many people from church were visiting me at home and she made that quite clear whilst she was still living with me, the only way I can describe it is that she must have felt challenged about how things had worked out and one thing was for sure she did not like being challenged. Over the time that we were still living under the same roof my wife had gone from just going out on Friday evenings to going out every evening, she was only a phone call away and always said that if their was a problem I must call her and she would come straight home. Their was always some friend or other that she was going to see for an hour, not this man that she was still seeing, however one day she was completely tripped up by one of her friends. I had needed to go out shopping and while I was out I bumped into one of her friends who she had apparently seen the night before, I asked her if she had a nice time with my wife the night before to which she replied "how can I have done when you don't let her go out". That told me all that I needed to know, that even to her friends my wife was telling lies about me and it no longer surprised me to hear that she was not being truthful, I just felt sad that she felt that she had to continue trying to cover up the truth.

Having to live under the same roof with a woman who was constantly not being truthful and who could blow up at any moment and make life miserable was not easy for me and my prayers at that time were all about her finally being given the green light to go and get the keys to her own house. In Late November my prayers were answered and my wife finally got the keys to her new home. She was worried about the whole move, she had little money to be able to carpet her house or decorate. So I told her that as long as she saved the money that I was giving her each week whatever she had at the time of her house move I would double to help her out, for me I was not doing this as a way of blessing my wife but as a way of blessing my children.

One other problem did present itself through her leaving the problem of her managing to move furniture and all her belongings. I felt awful asking my friends in church to help to move her but found that they were in fact willing to help and did it to help me and to bless me. It is something that has always weighed heavy on my heart that they did this as an act of kindness towards me. Not many of them knew what had been going on the whole time and I am sure that to find that we were splitting up was something of a shock to them. But Gods grace I knew was with them in the very fact that they helped that day and gave their blessing. My mum had continued to visit me and each week she would come and tell me how friends of hers had been giving her things for me to have, lots of things had been to her for me from furniture to general household things. I had told my wife to take most of the things from our house, and when the guys from church moved her furniture and things out, the house did for a couple of hours anyway look very bare. Peter and Jane had also managed to get me a couple of leather recliner chairs for my living room and just a couple of hours later my home looked like a home again.

One thing that was really saddening was the fact that I was now alone after everybody had gone, it was just me and my little home. My mum was now my carer but those first few nights of being alone and feeling like I had lost my children all over again was very difficult to take. Losing my family in this way was really hurting, but God was still telling me that it was something that had to happen, God just continually told me that I must trusty him.

PSALM 91 VERSE 2, I will say of the Lord, he is my refuge and my fortress: in him will I trust.

Again though the support and love continued to be poured out into my life by those closest to me and although things were tough I was still receiving a great amount of blessing. Barry and Lisa came to see me the week after my wife had left and they brought a bed settee that they no longer needed, Barry was still at a point where doing things like putting furniture together was still difficult for him, so when Peter came that next week he put it together for me. God continually knew what I needed and friends were often just popping in to see me in the weeks after my wife had left. One thing I did know though was that I was going to have to embrace the solitude and loneliness and make it a friend otherwise it could eat me alive and I was sure the Devil wanted that to happen, but God was with me through it all and gave me great courage and strength.

On the physical side of things it was a while before the community physio team were able to come and see me and I had been home for about four weeks when they made their first visit. Having physio again really helped me to focus again on getting better, my progress since leaving hospital had slowed down quite dramatically but now that I was receiving physio I did begin to see signs of improvement again. I also began to have hydrotherapy at the local hospital every Thursday morning and being able to do that again really helped me to loosen off. My body having not had the same level of intensive treatment since leaving hospital had stiffened up and I found myself in pain more often.

My physical improvement was still painfully slow but I was at least improving. Physically today I still have some severe weakness and still do require help with many things, I have found it frustrating to have the knowledge of how to do things like DIY but not be able to do it because of my bodily weakness. The upshot of even these frustrations is that I do feel blessed by God indeed, though life can be a struggle God is always there.

All through my darkest months God continued to give me his love, one particular evening I had just gotten to the top of the stairs on my stair lift and transferred into my wheelchair when I broke down sobbing in tears, the pain of everything I had gone through just came pouring out and as I sobbed I called out to God telling him that I could not do this on my own and that I wanted him to take away my pain. Guillain-Barre syndrome is one of the most emotional illnesses to go through it is truly a roller-coaster of experiences and emotions, without God I am sure I would never have gotten through it and dealt with my marriage break up too. I eventually settled down and went to bed but was woken at two in the morning by God, he told me to read the book of James. At first I protested to God that it was two in the morning and could I not read it in the morning, "no God said". So I put my little bedside lamp on and began to read, nothing jumped out at me in the first few lines of James, and I even said to God that nothing had jumped out at me, God came back and said to me "Jez you know better than that read on". JAMES 1 VERSES 2-4, Consider it pure joy, my brothers whenever you face trials of many kinds, because you know that the testing of your faith develops perseverance. Perseverance must finish its work so that you may be mature and complete not lacking anything. I have to say that I almost laughed out loud, but with a look towards the heavens I said "well got me there God". Considering my sufferings as pure joy at that time had been the very last thing that I had been doing, and it was not that I should enjoy being in pain but that I should in Christ. What I felt God was telling me was that I must face my sufferings head on and not hide away from them, but that I must put on the full armour of God. I read the whole book of James that night, one small book but oh boy so much teaching on how to live our lives, submitting to God, patience in suffering etc, all ending with the most powerful ingredient PRAYER!

Over the course of the next few days God continued to speak to me and gave me another piece of scripture that he told me was linked to what I had read in James.

2 CORINTHIANS 1 VERSES 3-4, Blessed be God, even the father of our Lord Jesus Christ, the father of mercies and the God of all comfort. Who comforteth us in all our tribulations, that we be able to comfort them which are in any trouble, by the comfort wherewith we ourselves are comforted of God.

God giving me these words told me that although there was nowhere for me to hide from my pain he was going to be there comforting me. It just brought me to a place where again I felt in awe of how great and wonderful our God is, his love continued to pour into my life, and he wants us to take that step of faith.

CONCLUSION

I have suffered on so many fronts, losing my health to losing my family and all the pain that that caused me. I spent a whole year and more seemingly holding on through the worst storm I have ever been in. Physically there is still a long way to go and a long road is still before me but I know that God is not finished with healing me. Physically my recovery has been very slow and frustrating and I am sure that my frustration has shown itself in the pages of this book, however I can clearly say that I would not be where I am today without my faith in God. One Sunday members of my church prayed for me because I had just had results that showed that their was no nerve activity in my legs below my knee's and that according to the doctors showed that I did have nerve damage in my legs, however a week after their prayers for me God gave me the strength to walk into church on my crutches. I had been able for some weeks to walk short distances around my home on my crutches with splints controlling the position of my feet so that I did not drag my toes on the floor. Although my lower legs were not healed of their weakness God gave me the strength to walk further than I had ever walked before, and for me that told me that without prayer we can not overcome or expect to see positive results. Prayer is always the answer as is Jesus! I still find today that I have to be very careful with how much I do on any given day as busy days do result in me being very fatigued. My energy levels do dip quite badly, living with disabilities does mean doing things differently and adapting and I have found that every day has its own set of challenges where it comes to my physical weaknesses. However I have found that when I lean on God he always gives me enough strength for each day.

As for my marriage my wife moved in with the man with whom she committed adultery with and I fought God for so long over the fact that he was telling me to divorce her. When I finally listened to God and began divorce proceedings though, God came and comforted me again and blessed me for my faith and for just doing what he told me to do. I still see my children regularly and I have a wonderful relationship with them both, and God has given me closure over having to end my marriage and the strength to move on. Though my illness was horrendous enough in itself I can truly say that the emotional heartache I suffered was far worse. Much of this book has focused on the problems I faced with my wife but truly that has been what has hurt the most and where I needed to trust the Lord the most. Music has been a huge part of my recovery and it is something that I find great joy in doing, God has laid so many songs in my heart to sing and perform and some of them have such a personal message about my journey through the valley of the shadow of death. Some are just pure praise songs in worship to Jesus. God has been so gracious to me and given me a heart to sing these songs for other people, I don't count myself as the greatest in fact probably the lowest when it comes to my God given talents with music, but I know that God does want me to share the music that I make with others.

Peter being a man of many talents has built me a website on which to share the songs and the music that God has given me. Again God has put before me everything that I will ever need to sing and praise his name you can check out the website for yourself, my one hope is that people will just be blessed by the music that they find on it. The address is www.jezsmith.org.uk The first album I have put together is called walking in the light, I feel it is such a fitting album name when I think of all I have gone through but my main reason for that name is that I truly feel that my every day has been a walk of faith since I fell ill.

For me personally I have had a real (Job) like journey, I have endured real hardships that at times have seemed impossible to overcome. But with God as my shield and with complete faith in him I know that anything is possible to overcome. One piece of scripture that I often look to is GENESIS 50 VERSE 20, Ye thought evil against me, but God meant it unto good. The enemy intended all that I have gone through to break me and ruin me, but he does not see that when true faith is displayed and that we truly trust God. God will turn all that the enemy does around for good, he thought that he could break Job, and he thought that he could tempt Jesus and that when Jesus went to the cross that that was the end of him, I often look at that and can almost hear the devil saying "look he is finished," then hear Jesus say "it is finished".

My Job like journey is not over and there are still many obstacles for me to overcome but I am in no doubt that God is going to bless the second part of my life more than the first, all I can say to that is, AMEN. God took me to a place where my whole life was stripped away and I lost everything that before my illness I held dear. In all honesty I was a man who walked in his own strength. When my life was turned upside down and I had nothing else to hold on to God came and taught me the most valuable lesson I have ever had to learn. That lesson is to trust God and put my complete faith in him, I have faced the most daunting of trials and would not have come through any of them if it had not been for Jesus. God always gives us the strength to get through our daily trials and as I look back over what has happened to me I can tell you that I would not change a thing, God has made me the man that I am today and he is still teaching me so much.

My walk with God today is deeper than it has ever been and I know what it is like to be staring into a black hole and teetering on the edge, but when we have Jesus in our lives we have hope. So my prayer is that through reading this book you will find the strength and courage to carry on and trust God and not give in, even when the situation seems impossible because nothing is impossible for God, it is only impossible for man. To God be the glory great things he has done, I leave you with the beginning of psalm 27, The Lord is my light and my salvation.